Freshwater Boundaries Revisited

Freshwater Boundaries Revisited

Recent Developments in International River and Lake Delimitation

By

María Querol

BRILL

LEIDEN | BOSTON

Library of Congress Control Number: 2016954436

Typeface for the Latin, Greek, and Cyrillic scripts: "Brill". See and download: brill.com/brill-typeface.

ISBN 978-90-04-33792-3 (paperback)
ISBN 978-90-04-33793-0 (e-book)

Originally published as Volume 1(3) 2016, in *International Water Law*, DOI 10.1163/23529369-12340003.

This book is printed on acid-free paper and produced in a sustainable manner.

Contents

BRILL INTERNATIONAL WATER LAW 1.3 (2016) 1–89 BRP brill.com/brp

Freshwater Boundaries Revisited

Recent Developments in International River and Lake Delimitation

María Querol
Independent Legal Consultant – Ph.D. in International Law from the Graduate Institute of International and Development Studies – Former Associate Professor of International Law at Austral University (Buenos Aires)

Abstract

Although boundaries, including freshwater ones, are generally set by treaties concluded by the states concerned, interpretation of such agreements by the different states has varied, resulting in a number of disputes before international tribunals. The aim of this monograph is to describe and analyze the different methods applied in the delimitation of international rivers and lakes and the recent developments in this field. The monograph reassesses these diverse methods of boundary delimitation in view of the latest and abundant jurisprudence of the International Court of Justice and the tribunals under the aegis of the Permanent Court of Arbitration on the subject. The monograph also focuses on the influence of human considerations in the field under study and the legal consequences ensuing therefrom, in addition to drawing some conclusions regarding freshwater boundaries.

Keywords

Boundaries – delimitation – international lakes – international rivers – watercourses

Introduction

Rivers are inherently interesting. They mold landscapes, create fertile deltas, provide trade routes, a source for food and water; a place to wash and play; civilizations emerged next to rivers in China, India, Europe, Africa and the Middle East. They sustain life and bring death and destruction. They are ferocious at times; gentle at times. They are placid and mean. They trigger conflict and delineate boundaries. Rivers are the stuff

 | DOI 10.1163/23529369-12340003

> of metaphor and fable, painting and poetry. Rivers unite and divide—a thread that runs from source to exhausted release.[1]

Rivers—as well as lakes—indeed unite and divide. As a matter of fact, the above description applies to all international watercourses. International rivers and lakes unite inasmuch as they are shared natural resources or, more precisely, a natural resource to be shared.[2] Natural resources are those elements of nature that are susceptible to being taken and consequently modified. Water, soil and flora are natural resources. Shared natural resources are those natural resources which are under the jurisdiction of two or more states sharing the resource to the exclusion of any other state. It is the nature of things and not the will of states that determines the shared character of a natural resource. Shared natural resources are subject to the exclusive jurisdiction of the state in whose territory they lie.

In light of this natural characteristic which they possess, international watercourses have been qualified as natural boundaries. Although they are elements of nature, it is actually the consent of two or more states that erects them as international boundaries. From a legal standpoint, those natural elements will only amount to boundaries insofar as there is a legal norm that so prescribes. Thus, all boundaries are artificial as legal creations. International rivers and lakes divide as much as they unite. States take them as reference points to divide their respective sovereign territories.

In line with this view, one of the main features of state territory is that it is a limited spatial sphere of validity of legal norms. It is a specific legal order, which is valid in a certain space and at a certain time. International law determines the temporal and spatial sphere of validity of each one of the legal orders, which constitute the international community. In doing so, it ensures the co-existence in space and the continuity in time of a community of neighbouring states.[3]

International boundaries are mainly created by the consent of states, which is consent materialised in either treaty provisions or arbitral or judicial awards. International boundary rivers and lakes are not exempted from this rule.

When addressing international boundaries in general, it is important to distinguish between delimitation and demarcation. Delimitation consists of

---

1 Gargan, E., *A River's Tale: A Year at the Mekong* (New York: Knopf, 2002), p. 7.

2 Caflisch, L., 'Règles générales du droit des cours d'eaux internationaux', *Recueil des cours de l'Académie de droit international de la Haye*, Vol. 219 (1989-VII), p. 134.

3 Barberis, J., *El territorio del Estado y la soberanía territorial* (Buenos Aires: Ábaco, 2003), pp. 135–136.

the establishment of the boundaries of a state's territory, meaning the succession of extreme points of the sphere of validity of the legal norm that entitles the state to cede that territory in question. The act of delimiting a state's territory is a legal act, which implies the creation of one or more legal norms. It determines the spatial sphere of validity of the legal norms that constitute the legal order of a certain state. On the contrary, demarcation is a set of technical procedures by virtue of which the line created by the legal norm is actually established on the ground.[4]

Inasfar as they amount to "a watercourse, parts of which are situated in different States",[5] the uses of international watercourses by a riparian state are likely to affect the other co-riparian states. Reference here is made to international watercourses as comprising international rivers and lakes. Different rules are applicable to groundwater resources, which fall outside the scope of the present monograph. This precision made, it is necessary to specify the notions of international river, and international lake, respectively.

International rivers are those rivers which either flow across the territory of more than one state or act as boundaries between two or more states. These rivers may possess either a successive or a contiguous character. Successive rivers traverse one or more international boundaries; they cross the territory of more than one state. On the other hand, contiguous rivers are those that separate the territory of two states.[6] An international river can thus be defined as that which either passes through the territory of two or more states or constitutes a boundary between them.[7] In this respect, Chile has recently instituted proceedings before the International Court of Justice against Bolivia with regard to a *Dispute over the Status and Use of the Waters of the Silala*. Whereas Bolivia denies the international character of this watercouse and

4 In this regard, see the Arbitral Award of 21 October 1994 in the case of *Laguna del Desierto*, between Argentina and Chile, para. 67.

5 Cf. Article 2(b) of the UN Convention on the Non-Navigational Uses of International Watercourses, adopted on 21 May 1997.

6 As a matter of fact, it may well occur that the same river corresponds to both categories depicted above. Such is the case with the Danube, which right from its source is a successive river (between Germany and Austria), then it turns into a contiguous one (between Slovakia and Hungary), to become again successive (when leaving Hungarian territory) and later on becomes contiguous again (between Croatia and Serbia, the latter and Romania, and finally between Romania and Bulgaria), and finally it recovers its successive character when it gets into Romanian territory, to end up being a contiguous river between Romania and Ukraine before flowing into the Black Sea.

7 Barberis, J. A., *Los recursos naturales compartidos entre Estados y el derecho internacional* (Madrid: Tecnos, 1979), p. 15.

proclaims its full sovereignty over its waters, Chile has requested the Court to adjuge and declare that ["t]he Silala River system, together with the subterranean portions of its system, is an international watercourse, the use of which is governed by customary international law".[8] In accordance with Chile's claim, the nature of the Silala River as an international watercourse was never disputed until 1999, when Bolivia started claiming its waters as exclusively Bolivian. In its Application, Chile argues that the Silala River originates from groundwater springs in Bolivian territory "at a few kilometres north-east of the Chile-Bolivia international boundary", and that the river then flows across the border into Chilean territory where it "receives additional waters from various springs (...) before it reaches the Inacaliri River".[9] In addition, Chile invokes the Treaty of Peace and Friendship of 20 October 1904, which established the boundary between the two states. On that occasion, both states adopted a map, which depicts the "Río Silala" as crossing the boundary between Bolivia and Chile, between point 15 (Cerro Silala) and point 16 (Cerro Inacaliri) of that boundary.[10] Consequently, Chile asserts its right to the reasonable and equitable utilization of that river's waters.

As regards international lakes, they comprise both those lakes whose hydrological basin is common to more than one state, and those other lakes that are cut in some way or another by a boundary between more than one state.[11] The

8 Ministerio de relaciones exteriores de la República de Chile, *Application Instituting Proceedings*, 6 June 2016, p. 11, para. 50(a). In addition, Chile requests the Court to declare that: "(b) Chile is entitled to the equitable and reasonable use of the waters of the Silala River system in accordance with customary international law; (c) Under the standard of equitable and reasonable utilization, Chile is entitled to its current use of the waters of the Silala River; (d) Bolivia has an obligation to take all appropriate measures to prevent and control pollution and other forms of harm to Chile resulting from its activities in the vicinity of the Silala River; (e) Bolivia has an obligation to cooperate and to provide Chile with timely notification of planned measures which may have an adverse effect on shared water resources, to exchange data and information and to conduct where appropriate an environmental impact assessment, in order to enable Chile to evaluate the possible effects of such planned measures, obligations that Bolivia has breached" (Ibid.). http://www.icj-cij.org/docket/index.php?p1=3&p2=1&k=74&case=162&code=chb&p3=0. Accessed on 10 June 2016.

9 Ibid., p. 3, para. 10.

10 Ibid., p. 4, para. 15.

11 These latter ones have also been named boundary lakes, in order to distinguish them from international lakes. Thus, international lakes would be tantamount to a *genus*, out of which boundary lakes ('lacs-frontière') would be a *species*. Pondaven, Ph., *Les lacs-frontière* (Paris: Pedone, 1972), p. 6 et seq.

subject of the present monograph is circumscribed around international rivers and lakes of a contiguous nature.

Despite the attempt made in doctrine to assimilate rivers and lakes, they are indeed distinct from a geological and hydrographical standpoint. Such a misconception is usually based on the fact that many lakes are part of a river system taken as a whole. There are in limnology two decisive distinguishing elements of lakes: first, lakes are tantamount to a mass of water with a horizontal surface.[12] Second, the relation between the daily amount of water flow and water retained is much lower than a unit. These particular features of lakes enable them to be distinguished from the phenomeon of water accumulation, which takes place in dams.

Lakes should further be distinguished from seas. The international law consequences ensuing from such a distinction are crucial since they will determine the application of the norms appertaining to the Law of the Sea in one case or of those on the delimitation and uses of international watercourses in the other. In this regard, the distinguishing element will be provided by the level of the waters under consideration. Whilst the level of waters in lakes does not correspond to that of seas, every expanse of water situated at altitude zero is, no doubt, a sea.[13] Despite its being otherwise advanced, the degree of saltiness of the waters does not enable any distinction in this regard.[14] Actually, there are seas whose degree of saltiness is rather low[15] and large lakes which have turned out to be extremely salty.[16]

The aim of the present monograph is an analysis of the different systems currently applied in the delimitation of international boundary rivers and lakes in the light of the latest developments in this field. Taking as a basis the previous work of this author on the subject at the Hague Academy of International Law,[17] the existing diverse methods of international watercourse delimitation will be reassessed in view of the most recent and abundant jurisprudence of the International Court of Justice and the tribunals under the aegis of the

12 Ibid., p. 11.

13 Ibid., p. 12.

14 Cf. Daillier, P., & Pellet, A. (eds.), Nguyen Quoc Dinh, *Droit international public* (Paris: L.G.D.J., 1999), p. 1180.

15 Such is the case of the Baltic Sea. Cf. Schröter, F., 'La délimitation des lacs internationaux: essai d'une typologie', *Annuaire français de droit international*, Vol. 40 (1995), p. 911.

16 Among other examples, see the case of the Great Salt Lake. Cf. Pondaven, supra, note 11, pp. 12–13.

17 Querol, M., 'Rethinking International Rivers and Lakes as Boundaries', *in*, Boisson de Chazournes, L. & Salman, M. A. S. (eds.), *Water Resources and International Law* (The Hague: Hague Academy of International Law & Martinus Nijhoff, 2005), pp. 97–132.

Permanent Court of Arbitration on the subject. In fact, the last few years have witnessed the production by these tribunals of abundant *dicta* where the subject of international river and lake delimitation has been addressed either directly or indirectly.

In addition, this analysis will focus on the influence of human considerations in the field under study and of the legal consequences ensuing therefrom. As a matter of fact, the human factor has been progressively gaining momentum and is nowadays uncontestably instilled within the international legal order. Water is essential to human life and, as such, states have sought to assure its access when delimiting their respective territories. As will be duly noticed, this is also true in cases of state succession.[18] In this respect, in most cases of state succession, the newly created state has taken into consideration access to fresh water when agreeing with its neighbouring states the resulting international boundaries. Hence, the impact of the above-mentioned considerations in international river and lake delimitation must also be addressed. In this respect, the question as to the source of the validity of the international norms regulating the determination of boundaries in international watercourses comes to light. In sum, both the nature and content of the existing norms in the field of international river and lake delimitation will be revisited.

Part 1: An Analysis of Possible Delimitation Methods

I *General Remarks*

Since international rivers flow through the territory of more than one state and international lakes are cut by a boundary between more than one state, the

18 This statement can also be analyzed in the light of state succession. In fact, after the unification of Germany in 1990, this state confirmed its former boundary with Poland at the Oder-Neisse (Treaty of 12 September 1990 between Germany and 'the Four', *Revue générale de droit international public* (1990), pp. 1166–1170). A similar idea was presented after the independence of Namibia on 31 March 1990. The Namibian Constitution foresees the application of the former boundary treaties, which were concluded by Germany as a colonial power. As a result of this, several years ago a controversy arose between Namibia and Botswana on the interpretation of one of these treaties which regulated the boundary between both states. For the development of this case see infra, p. 42. For a further analysis of the recent cases of state succession and their consequences as regards international boundaries, see Márquez Carrasco, M. C., 'Régimes de frontières et autres régimes territoriaux face à la succession d'Etats', *in*, Eisemann, M. & Koskenniemi, M. (eds.), *State Succession: Codification Tested against the Facts* (The Hague: Martinus Nijhoff, 2000), p. 549 et seq.

uses of riparian states in the watercourse in question will definitely have an impact outside their boundaries and within the territory of their fellow co-riparians.[19] The aims of these uses of international rivers and lakes are as numerous as they are diverse. They range primarily from domestic and sanitary—with regard to the human need to have access to fresh water, to irrigation (above all in agricultural practices), navigation for communication and commercial reasons, hydroelectric power and fishing for subsistence purposes—just to name the main ones.[20] Access to international rivers and lakes becomes therefore essential for the well-being of states and their inhabitants.

The purpose of this section is to address the existing systems of delimitation for international rivers and lakes through the lens of the utility and applicability of those systems. These criteria are indeed the guiding elements in the choice by state agents and boundary commissioners of a particular type of boundary line, over other types, to be applied to delimit a certain international watercourse. Indeed, the evaluation of the advantages of the most suitable method of delimitation for a particular international watercourse should be provided by both the natural characteristics of that watercourse and the main uses contemplated by its riparian states.[21]

As a result, the relationship of the rules applicable to freshwater delimitation and those regulating the uses of transboundary watercourses comes to light. As advanced above, international watercourses can serve multiple functions. Indeed, they unite and divide. They can form the international boundaries between two or more states. At the same time, some international watercourses allow for navigational and non-navigational uses, the former being of crucial use for states with no direct access to the sea.

As regards the rules on navigation of international fresh watercourses, passenger and merchandise transport was considered of vital importance during the nineteenth and at the beginning of the twentieth centuries, mainly for commercial and strategic reasons. The Final Act of the Congress of Vienna (15 June 1815), which put an end to the Napoleonic Wars,[22] opened the rivers

---

19 Cf. Barberis, Julio A., 'Bilan de recherches de la section de langue française du Centre d'Etude et de Recherche de l'Académie', *Droit et obligations des pays riverains des fleuves internationaux*, Centre d'Etude et de Recherche de droit international et de relations internationales (La Haye: Académie de droit international, 1990), pp. 18–20.

20 Barberis, J., supra, note 7, p. 15.

21 Cf. Bouchez, L.J., 'The Fixing of Boundaries in International Boundary Rivers', *International & Comparative Law Quarterly*, Vol. 12 (July 1963), p. 797 et seq.

22 Parry, C., *Consolidated Treaty Series*, Vol. 64, p. 67 et seq.

of the state parties to vessels of their respective *pavillions* to freely navigate for commercial purposes.[23] Such rules gradually extended throughout the rest of Europe, ensuring the freedom of navigation to all states—be they riparian or not—along the rivers of the entire continent. Furthermore, this rule on freedom of navigation was transposed to the River Congo (Zaire) by virtue of the 1885 Berlin Congress, and became progressively applied to other African fresh watercourses.

The opening of navigable watercourses of Europe to all nations was definitively guaranteed in the 1919 Versailles Peace Treaty[24] and in the 1921 Barcelona Statute.[25] The consecutive reaffirmation of the principle of freedom of navigation in fresh watercourses in treaties since 1815 has been recognized by international jurisprudence as evidence of the existence of a customary norm in this regard. Along this line, in the *Territorial Jurisdiction of the International Commission of the River Oder* case, the Permanent Court of International Justice refers to international river law and defines it as the law "laid down by the Act of the Congress of Vienna of June 9th, 1815, and applied or developed by subsequent conventions".[26] Inspired by this same principle, the Institute of International Law approved a resolution regulating navigation in international rivers.

The clauses on freedom of navigation in international rivers in the treaties mentioned above possessed a programmatic character.[27] As a result, freedom of navigation could not be imposed as a general rule on every state of the international community unless it so consented.[28] It would only be applicable to European rivers.[29] Precisely, none of the states sharing the large international river basins of Latin America ratified those agreements. In fact, the regulation of navigation in those Latin American river basins has acquired a strictly territorial character.[30] Accordingly, the vessels of a riparian state of an international fresh watercourse can only navigate freely in the section of the

23 See Articles 108 to 117 of this instrument, ibid., p. 490 et seq.

24 Martens, G. F., *Nouveau Recueil Général des Traités*, 3ème, Série, Vol. 11, p. 300 et seq.

25 *League of Nations Treaty Series*, Vol. 7, p. 35 et seq.

26 *P.C.I.J. Reports, Series A, No. 23*, p. 27.

27 Caflisch, supra, note 2, p. 117.

28 Mubiala, M., *L'évolution du droit des cours d'eau internationaux à la lumière de l'expérience africaine, notamment dans le Bassin du Congo/Zaïre* (Paris: Presses Universitaires de France, 1995), p. 31.

29 Cf. Vitanyi, B. K. J., 'Navigation on Rivers and Canals', *Encyclopedia of Public International Law*, Vol. 11, p. 237.

30 Barberis, J., 'Les règles spécifiques du droit international en Amérique Latine', *Recueil des cours de l'Académie de droit international de la Haye*, Vol. 235 (1992-IV), pp. 183–184. See

watercourse lying within its territory. They are impaired from freely navigating along the waters of international watercourses situated within the territory of other states unless these latter so consent through a treaty or by unilateral act. Indeed, this is a particularity of navigation in Latin America.

The particularities of the rules of navigation on international watercourses affect in turn those of boundary delimitation. The prevailing method of delimitation chosen for a certain watercourse may vary according to the region where that watercourse is situated and owing to the importance of navigation for both riparian and non-riparian states. Such a statement especially holds true with regards to Latin American fresh watercourses. Indeed, certain methods of delimitation, such as the line at the single riverbank, result in principle in the complete exclusion of one of the riparian states from accessing the watercourse in question and even from navigating along its waters. Nonetheless, as will be analyzed below, the only remaining case of such a boundary is that of the San Juan River, which lies within Nicaraguan territory. Nonetheless, in this case, Costa Rica, the neighbouring riparian state, has been assured access to its waters by virtue of the boundary treaty. If it had not, this state would be impaired from navigating the waters of the San Juan River unless so authorized by Nicaragua.

As regards non-navigational uses, the particular features of each international watercourse and the diverse uses they can serve have resulted, in practice, in their regulation through bilateral agreements.[31] Irrespective of the particularity of each agreement, the practice of similar clauses of bilateral treaties on the exploitation of international watercourses has resulted in the emergence of a number of general customary norms,[32] which have been expressly incorporated in the 1997 Convention on the Non-Navigational Uses of International Watercourses.[33] The main substantive norms regulating the use

also Ruiz Fabri, H., 'Règles coutumières générales et droit international fluvial', *Annuaire français de droit international*, Vol. XXXVI (1990), p. 832.

31 Caponera favours the conclusion of particular agreements due to the specificity of each watercourse. Caponera, D., 'Patterns of Cooperation in International Water Law: Principles and Institutions', *in*, Utton, A. E. & Teclaff, L. A. (eds.), *Transboundary Resources Law* (Boulder: Westview Press, 1987), p. 25.

32 Cf. Wolfrom, M. & Rousseau, Ch., *L'utilisation à des fins autres que la navigation des eaux des fleuves, des lacs et canaux internationaux* (Paris: Pedone, 1964), p. 142. Hayton, R. D., 'The Formation of the Customary Rules of International Drainage Basins', *in*, Garretson, A. H. et al. (eds.), *The Law of International Drainage Basins* (New York: Oceana Publications, 1967), p. 834 et seq.

33 Salman argues that there are five main contentions justifying the former reluctance of states to ratify this Convention during the first years following its adoption. First, there

of an international watercourse are the prohibition to cause significant harm to another state and the equitable and reasonable utilization of its waters.[34]

The activities of a riparian state on an international watercourse can alter the latter's quality, quantity or level. Whereas these alterations generally affect downstream states, they may well affect the upper riparian states also,[35] if the downstream riparian state dams a river, for instance.[36] Hence, the effects of the activities of a riparian state on any of the different elements of an international watercourse—its course, water level, volume or quality of its water—may be detrimental to another riparian.

Water pollution is a particular way of causing significant harm to another riparian state. Thus, the prohibition against polluting international watercourses amounts to a special application of the general customary norm prohibiting the causing of significant harm to another state.[37] States are

---

is the relationship between the principle of equitable and reasonable utilization and the obligation not to cause harm. Second, upper riparians argue that the notification process gives downstream riparians a veto power over their projects. Third, existing agreements would not be appropriately addressed or fully recognized. In addition, there is a weak dispute settlement mechanism with no established binding compulsory method. Finally, the broad definition of the term 'watercourse state' as including regional economic integration organizations is regarded as recognizing their international legal personality. Salman, S. M. A., 'The United Nations Watercourses Convention Ten Years Later: Why Has Its Entry into Force Proven Difficult?', *Water International*, Vol. 31 (2007), pp. 8–11.

34 International case law is another fertile field for finding such general norms. The resolutions of international organs, such as the United Nations General Assembly and ECOSOC, and scientific institutions, inasmuch as they prove existing *opinio juris* in this area of international law, are also relevant, particularly the 1966 Helsinki Rules on the Uses of the Waters of International Rivers and the Berlin Rules on Water Resources of the International Law Association. Cf. Helsinki Rules on the Uses of International Rivers, *International Law Association*, Vol. 52 (1967), pp. 447–533. For the Berlin Rules, see http://www.ila-hq.org/en/committees/index.cfm/cid/32. Accessed on 2 April 2016.

35 This possibility is specifically foreseen in Annex II of the Tripartite Agreement on the Itaipú Dam of 19 October 1979 between Argentina, Brazil and Paraguay, *International Legal Materials*, Vol. 19 (1980), p. 617.

36 This is the case of the construction of the Libby dam in the Kootenay River, a tributary of the Columbia River. Johnson, R. W., 'The Columbia Basin', *in*, Garretson, supra, note 32, pp. 198–200.

37 This view is confirmed by the arbitral award in the *Trail Smelter* case: "[U]nder the principles of international law, as well as the law of the United States, no State has the right to use or permit the use of its territory in such a manner as to cause injury by fumes in or to the territory of another or the properties or persons therein, when the case is of serious consequence and the injury is established by clear and convincing evidence". *United Nations Reports of International Arbitral Awards*, Vol. III, p. 1905, at p. 1965. The same idea

also obliged under general international law to prevent with due diligence the occurrence of a serious level of harm by pollution of international watercourses.[38] In its advisory opinion on the *Legality of the Threat or Use of Nuclear Weapons*, the International Court of Justice declared that:

> [t]he existence of the general obligation of States to ensure that activities within their jurisdiction and control respect the environment of other States or of areas beyond national control is now part of the corpus of international law relating to the environment.[39]

The obligation not to cause significant harm to another riparian state is a particular application of the prohibition of abuse of rights in neighbourly relations among states. This principle is embodied in the Roman maxim *sic utere tuo ut alienum non laedas* (use what is yours in such a manner that you do not harm others).[40]

No change in a watercourse is illegal in itself unless it causes 'significant' harm to another state.[41] The arbitral award of 16 November 1957 in the *Lac Lanoux* case between France and Spain stated that there is a principle

---

lies at the basis of the *Corfu Channel* case, where the International Court of Justice named among certain general well-recognized principles "every State's obligation not to allow knowingly its territory to be used for acts contrary to the rights of other States". *Corfu Channel case (United Kingdom v. Albania), Merits, Judgment of 9th April 1949, I.C.J. Reports 1949*, p. 4, at p. 22. This is consistent with Principle 21 of the Stockholm Declaration on the Human Environment adopted on 16 June 1972. United Nations Document A/CONF.48/14. For an opposite view, see Sette-Camara, J., 'Pollution of International Rivers', *Recueil des cours de l'Académie de droit international de la Haye*, Vol. 186 (1984-III), p. 163.

38 Yasuhiro, Sh., 'Some Reflections on the Relationship Between the Principle of Equitable Utilization of International Watercourses and the Obligation Not to Cause Transfrontier Pollution Harm', *Asian Yearbook of International Law*, Vol. 9 (2004), pp. 148–150.

39 *Legality of the Threat or Use of Nuclear Weapons, Advisory Opinion, I.C.J. Reports 1996*, p. 226, at pp. 241–242.

40 Caflisch states that this rule is applicable to international watercourses, land and maritime territory and the aerial space of states. Caflisch, L., 'Sic utere tuo ut alienum non laedas: Règle prioritaire ou élément servant à mesurer le droit de participation équitable et raisonnable à l'utilisation d'un cours d'eau international ?', *in*, Von Ziegler, A. & Burckhardt, Th. (eds.), *Internationales Recht auf See und Binnengewässern : Festschrift für Walter Müller* (Zürich: Schulthess, 1993), p. 28.

41 Andrassy, J., 'L'utilisation des eaux des basins fluviaux internationaux', *Revue Égyptienne de Droit International*, Vol. 16 (1960), p. 37 and Colliard, C.-A., 'Évolution et aspects actuels du régime juridique des fleuves internationaux', *Recueil des cours de l'Académie de droit international de la Haye*, Vol. 125 (1968-III), p. 378 et seq.

prohibiting the upstream riparian state to alter the waters of a river in any way that seriously harms the downstream riparian state.[42]

The prohibition to cause significant harm only comprises injuries caused by human acts. Therefore, states are not obliged to modify the natural conditions of an international watercourse or to prevent the natural alterations it may suffer.[43] Whilst Article 7 of the UN Watercourses Convention contains a prohibition to cause significant harm, it does not provide a definition of that notion.[44] Significant harm is not so much qualified as harm on a considerable scale, but what is considered objectively assessable damage. The word 'significant' qualifies harm by raising the level of tolerance in the exploitation of international watercourses.[45]

The right of states to an equitable and reasonable use of international watercourses is the logical consequence of the prohibition to cause significant harm.[46] States generally try to use the waters of their international watercourses to obtain the maximum benefit with the least inconvenience. States have the same right of access to the benefits that may be gained from the

42 *United Nations Reports of International Arbitral Awards*, Vol. XII, p. 304, at p. 308. In its memorial in the *Pulp Mills* case, Argentina claimed a violation of the general obligation prohibiting significant harm in the use of an international watercourse by the construction and operation of a pulp mill on the border of the Uruguay River. Cf. paragraph 8.19 of the Memorial at www.icj-cij.org. Accessed on 2 January 2016.

43 Cf. Barberis, supra, note 19, p. 34.

44 Article 7 prescribes: "1. Watercourse States shall, in utilizing an international watercourse in their territories, take all appropriate measures to prevent the causing of significant harm to other watercourse States. 2. Where significant harm nevertheless is caused to another watercourse State, the States whose use causes such harm shall, in the absence of agreement to such use, take all appropriate measures, having due regard for the provisions of articles 5 and 6 (on equitable and reasonable utilisation), in consultation with the affected State, to eliminate or mitigate such harm and, where appropriate, to discuss the question of compensation".

45 Pannatier, S., 'La protection des eaux douces', *in, Le droit international face à l'éthique et à la politique de l'environnement* (Genève: Georg Éditeur, 1996), p. 63.

46 Barberis, J., Armas Pfirter, F. & Querol, M., 'Aplicación de principios de derecho internacional en la administración de ríos compartidos. Argentina con Paraguay y Uruguay', *in, El derecho de aguas en Ibeoramérica y España: Cambio y modernización en el inicio del tercer milenio* (Madrid: Civitas, 2002), Vol. 2, p. 77. Fitzmaurice refers to the 'holistic approach' that both general norms reflect concerning the use of international waterways. Fitzmaurice, M., 'General Principles Governing the Cooperation Between States in Relation to Non-Navigational Uses of International Watercourses', *Yearbook of International Environmental Law*, Vol. 14 (2003), p. 44; Vitányi, B., *The International Regime of River Navigation* (Alphen aan den Rijn: Sitjhoff & Noordhoff, 1979), pp. 345–346.

exploitation of the waterway. However, this does not entail equal rights of participation.[47] 'Equitable' does not mean identical. The International Court of Justice underlined this idea in the *Black Sea Delimitation* case, where, citing its previous *dicta* on the matter, it stated:

> The Court further observes that for the purposes of this final exercise in the delimitation process the calculation of the relevant area does not purport to be precise and is approximate. The object of delimitation is to achieve a delimitation that is equitable, not an equal apportionment of maritime areas (*North Sea Continental Shelf* (*Federal Republic of Germany/Denmark; Federal Republic of Germany/Netherlands*), *Judgment, I.C.J. Reports 1969*, p. 22, para. 18; *Maritime Delimitation in the Area between Greenland and Jan Mayen* (*Denmark* v. *Norway*), *Judgment, I.C.J. Reports 1993*, p. 67, para. 64).[48]

The notion of equitable utilization conveys the idea that states participate in the benefits proportionally to allow each of them to satisfy its needs.

The concept of equitable and reasonable use can be viewed from two standpoints: the reasonable and equitable share of benefits, on the one hand, and the equitable and reasonable exploitation of international watercourses, on the other. The notion of an equitable and reasonable share in the beneficial uses of the waters of an international watercourse is flexible since it takes into account the particularities of each case where this norm is applied. Article v of the Helsinki Rules provides a non-exhaustive list of factors in the light of which the share of each state can be considered. The list contains three types of elements. First, natural factors, such as the geography of the basin and its climate. Historical considerations are also pertinent, for instance, prior uses of the watercourse under consideration. Finally, the socio-economic needs of the riparian states—and those states' capacity to find substitute resources (and the cost of those resources)—are germane to the decision on the share of each state of the benefits of the international watercourse.[49] In the consideration of

47 Caflisch, supra, note 2, pp. 148–149.

48 *Maritime Delimitation in the Black Sea* (*Romania* v. *Ukraine*), *Judgment, I.C.J. Reports 2009*, p. 61, at p. 100, para. 111.

49 Paragraph 2 of Article v of the Helsinki Rules prescribes: "Relevant factors which are to be considered include, but are not limited to: 1. The geography of the basin, including in particular the extent of the drainage area in the territory of each basin State; 2. The hydrology of the basin, including in particular the contribution of water by each basin State; 3. The climate affecting the basin; 4. The past utilization of the waters of the basin, including

these factors, existing prior uses do not amount to an acquired right of the state profiting from it.[50] Hence, the position of prevailing uses in each international watercourse depends on the circumstances of the case.[51] Article 14 of the 2004 Berlin Rules adds a very important exception in this regard: in determining an equitable and reasonable use, preference shall be given to the allocation of waters to satisfy vital human needs. In line with this idea, Article 6 of the UN Convention on the Non-Navigational Uses of International Watercourses makes reference to the population dependent on the watercourse in each watercourse state as a factor to be taken into account. In addition, it prescribes that in determining what is a reasonable and equitable use, all relevant factors are to be considered together and a conclusion reached on the basis of the whole. Article 10 of the same instrument states that, in the event of a conflict between uses of an international watercourse, special regard shall be accorded to the requirements of vital human needs.

The International Court of Justice has linked the notion of equitable and reasonable share to that of proportionality in the *Gabčíkovo-Nagymaros Project* case:

> The Court considers that Czechoslovakia, by unilaterally assuming control of a shared resource, and thereby depriving Hungary of its right to an equitable and reasonable share of the natural resources of the

in particular existing utilization; 5. The economic and social needs of each basin State; 6. The population dependent on the waters of the basin in each basin State; 7. The comparative costs of alternative means of satisfying the economic and social needs of each basin State; 8. The availability of other resources; 9. The avoidance of unnecessary waste in the utilization of waters of the basin; 10. The practicability of compensation to one or more of the co-basin States as a means of adjusting conflicts among uses; and 11. The degree to which the needs of a basin State may be satisfied, without causing substantial injury to a co-basin State".

50 Brown Weiss argues that the flexibility of the norm of equitable and reasonable utilization is also its nemesis "since allocations of water could seemingly be reconsidered at any point in response to more users. This can create problems for water users in arid areas". Brown Weiss, E., 'The Evolution of International Water Law', *Recueil des cours de l'Académie de droit international de la Haye*, Vol. 331 (2007), p. 202.

51 Tarlock and Wouters address the application of shared benefits as a strategy for the development of international water basins. They find three possible benefits that can flow from an international watercourse: better ecosystem management, river services such as hydroelectric power, and the achievement of regional water security through cost sharing. They conclude that only river services determine current state practice. Tarlock, A. D. & Wouters, P., 'Are Shared Benefits of International Waters an Equitable Apportionment?', *Colorado Journal of International Environmental Law and Policy*, Vol. 18 (2007), p. 533.

> Danube—with the continuing effects of the diversion of these waters on the ecology of the riparian area of the Szigetkoz—failed to respect the proportionality which is required by international law.[52]

The idea beneath the rule of reasonable and equitable use is that of maximal exploitation of the international watercourse without endangering its possible future use.[53] For instance, it would not be reasonable to use a river with an abundant flow exclusively for the practice of aquatic sports or to irrigate very small land surfaces.

In addition to the substantive norms described above, there is a procedural norm regulating the use of an international watercourse: the obligation to notify other riparian states of any work in the shared fresh watercourse that is likely to cause significant harm. Riparian states need to be able to assess if a planned measure in a certain international fresh watercourse is likely to cause significant harm or complies with an equitable and reasonable use of that watercourse. To do so, they need to be duly informed of all aspects of the projected work.

The obligation to notify other watercourse states of planned measures in the watercourse in question is foreseen by Part III of the UN Convention on the Non-Navigational Uses of International Watercourses. Article 11 regulates the exchange of information, consultation and, if necessary, the obligation to negotiate the possible effects of planned measures on the condition of an international watercourse. The regular exchange of data and information on the general conditions of the shared watercourse is foreseen by Article 9 of the same instrument. This norm establishes an obligation of means upon watercourse states: to employ its best efforts to provide that data to the requesting state. Once a state has been duly notified of a planned measure in a certain watercourse, it has from six and up to 12 months to evaluate it and reply. The principle of good faith encompasses the whole notification and consultation procedure in order to make operative the obligation to notify.

The moral value of justice lying at the basis of the notion of equity encroaches on international legal norms regulating both the delimitation and the management of international watercourses. This moral value is taken into account by the international legal order, which possesses a tool sufficiently within reach to prevent inequitable or unreasonable uses of international watercourses.

52 *Gabčíkovo-Nagymaros Project (Hungary* v. *Slovakia), Judgment, I.C.J. Reports 1997*, p. 7, at p. 56, para. 85.

53 Cf. Bourne, C. B., 'The Right to Utilize Waters of International Rivers', *Canadian Yearbook of International Law*, Vol. 3 (1965), p. 199.

The norm of equitable and reasonable use is not identical with decisions *ex aequo et bono* since it is a legal norm that prescribes resorting to equity in each particular case. As a result, the uses of international watercourses must comply with the conditions of the international legal norm, yet they must also be in line with the moral requirements of equity established by that norm. The same moral value is present in the current state of the law of transboundary watercourse delimitation, in the latter case in the form of distributive justice.

Forteau argues that the legal norm prescribing the equitable and reasonable use of transboundary fresh watercourses is applicable to fresh watercourses possessing an international character. However, these watercourses will be duly classified as international as a result of a delimitation operation that establishes the boundary between two riparian states in a certain fresh watercourse. Hence, it appears that freshwater delimitation must precede any definition on the legal regime regulating the uses of an international fresh watercourse. Nonetheless, the *raison d'être* behind the choice of a watercourse boundary is precisely the will of each of its co-riparian states to ensure access to its waters.[54] The interested parties actually always have in mind the different uses they envisage of the watercourse in question *at the time* when they are negotiating the delimitation and not after. As a result, the contemplated uses of a certain fresh watercourse undoubtedly condition the delimitation method adopted in practice.[55] Furthermore, since the principle of reasonable and equitable utilization is a norm of general international law, it is binding as such upon riparian states who intend to delimit their respective fresh watercourse boundaries. As such, it has to be taken into consideration during the delimitation process. Hence, when deliberating on the most convenient boundary line for a particular river, co-riparian states should take into account the natural properties of the watercourse in question on the one hand—its natural configuration and hydro-geological features—and, on the other hand, its main functions or the uses envisaged by those states.

54 This was expressly recognized by Judge Higgins in the *Kasikili/Sedudu Island* case, where she acknowledges that "(…) two things were important to Britain and Germany as they concluded the Treaty of 1890. The first was that they sought a clear delimitation of their spheres of interest in (inter alia) the north eastern sector of South West Africa. The second was that they supposed that this could be done in a way as to allow to each party the possibility of riverine access to the Zambezi". *Kasikili Sedudu Island* (*Botswana/Namibia*), *Judgment, Declaration of Judge Higgins, I.C.J. Reports 1999* (*II*), p. 1045, at p. 1114, para. 5.

55 Forteau, M., 'Délimitation à la rive, au thalweg, au milieu du chenal', *in*, Aurescu, B. & Pellet, A. (eds.), *Actualité du droit des fleuves internationaux* (Paris: Pedone, 2010), p. 32.

Having situated the law of freshwater boundary delimitation in the context of the main legal regimes applying to transboundary watercourses, it is important to bear in mind that the applicable rules on international river and lake delimitation possess a technical nature. They amount to technical standards at the service of riparian states faced with the task of delimiting their respective boundary watercourses.[56] Their source of validity being consensual, state practice is very diverse in this regard, as will be further examined. Furthermore, reference to these methods of delimitation in conventional clauses can prove to be both vague and ambiguous.

Some doctrinal voices postulate the existence of a customary norm in this field prescribing resort to the *thalweg* or main channel for navigable waterways, and to the median line for non-navigable ones.[57] It could also be argued to support this view that the *thalweg* is seldom applied in lakes due to the fact that more often than not they lack a navigable channel. One of the rare cases in this respect is that of the Mirim Lagoon, between Brazil and Uruguay.[58]

The above-mentioned factors forestall the identification of the material element of custom or a constant and uniform practice of riparian states in this regard. Even in the case of international lakes, it cannot be concluded that states have agreed on the application of a special method of delimitation. Thus, it is pointless to look for a psychological element or *opinio juris*. In the present state of international law, it is not possible to identify the existence of a customary norm prescibing resort to a particular system of delimitation of international watercourses. This conclusion, however, does not prejudge the possible existence of other norms with a different content with regard to the subject under analysis. Concerning their nature, such norms might also

56 In this sense, see Caflisch, L., 'The Law of International Waterways and its Sources', *in*, MacDonald, R. St.J. (ed.), *Essays in Honour of Wang Tieya* (Great Britain: Kluwer Academic Publishers, 1993), pp. 120–121. See also Ruiz Fabri, H., 'Règles coutumières générales et droit international fluvial', *Annuaire français de droit international*, Vol. 36 (1990), pp. 818–842. See also Schröter, F., 'Les systèmes de délimitation dans les fleuves internationaux', *Annuaire français de droit international*, Vol. 38 (1992), pp. 965–968.

57 Jennings R. & Watts, A., *Oppenheim's International Law*, Vol. 1, Parts 2–4 (London: Longman, 1992), pp. 664–665.

58 The Mirim Lagoon possesses in fact a navigable channel. The *thalweg* has been adopted as the boundary by virtue of Article 3 of the Treaty of 30 October 1909, which prescribes: "The new frontier shall traverse longitudinally Lake Mirim (...) by means of a broken line, defined by many straight lines as may be necessary to maintain the average distance between the principal points of the two shores, or, if the depth be insufficient, by as many straight lines as may be necessary to keep in the principal channel of the said lake (...) the deepest channel (...)", Parry, C., *Consolidated Treaty Series*, Vol. 209, p. 419 et seq.

be customary or even possess a different source of validity, as will be studied throughout this monograph.

II *No Man's Land or Condominium*

It seems paradoxical to start our analysis of the existing systems of delimitation with a legal figure that is seldom used, as is the case of condominium. Still, we believe that this is mainly due to the lack of a clear and specific definition of this legal construct and its features. In order to encourage its application, it is necessary to specify its constituent characteristics.

Unlike the case of shared natural resources where there is always a boundary delimiting territory among states—as with boundary lines on superficial freshwaters—in that of condominium there is no boundary in the river or lake in question. This type of boundary is made up of two boundaries, each of which arrives at the right and left riverbank respectively, thus leaving the watercourse in question under the sovereignty of both riparian states. In this regard, the very concept of condominium finds its root in the notion of natural boundary or *frontière naturelle*.[59] The only exception would be the case of a canalized river, where there has been human activity in the watercourse in question. There is actually no boundary line but a border area between the states concerned so it amounts to what is known as a *frontière espace*.[60] This is the reason why it has been also considered a 'no man's land'.

Generally, state territory is envisaged as appertaining to only one state. Nevertheless, condominium can be described as the hypothesis of a territory which belongs to two or more different states. Barberis found two concurring characteristics of condominium: a) the coincidence of a certain space as the territory of various states, meaning that states must be territorial sovereigns of such a space that they enjoy the faculty of ceding that territory to a third state; and b) the impossibility of the co-sovereign states to cede their rights to the territory in question to a third party without the consent of all the other parties.[61]

59 Cf. Caflisch, supra, note 2, pp. 67–68.

60 Caflisch, L., 'Essai de typologie des frontières fluviales', *in*, Aurescu, B. & Pellet, A. (eds.), *Actualité du droit des fleuves internationaux* (Paris: Pedone, 2010), p. 18.

61 Barberis, J. A., 'Quelques considérations sur le condominium en droit international public', *in*, Kohen, M. G. (ed.), *Promoting Justice, Human Rights and Conflict Resolution Through International Law: Liber Amicorum Lucius Caflisch* (Leiden: Martinus Nijhoff, 2007), p. 678 et seq.

Examples of this type of boundary go back in history[62] as far as the Middle Ages when it was recorded that the Rhine: "*ex una ripa Galliae, ex altera Germaniae limes* (*est*)".[63] Whilst most of the cases we find at present are maritime or fluvial in character, it is actually the case of the Faisan island or Ile de la Conférence between France and Spain that is the most well known. By virtue of the Treaty of 2 December 1856, both states agree that the said island, which is located in the Bidassoa River, belongs in an undivided manner to France and Spain.[64]

Moreover, the Moselle River amounts to a condominium along 36 kilometres between Germany and Luxembourg.[65] In addition, by virtue of the Treaty of 19 February 1957 between Bolivia and Peru, the use of the waters of Lake Titicaca presupposes "the indivisible and exclusive condominium", of both states over the lake.[66] Similarly, Article 2 of the 1973 Treaty on the Rio de la Plata establishes a band of exclusive jurisdiction for Argentina and Uruguay

62 In this sense, see the Treaty of Aix-la-Chapelle of 26 June 1816 between the Netherlands and Germany *in*, Martens, Ch. de, *Nouveau Recueil des Traités*, Vol. 3, p. 36. The said agreement was later confirmed on 8 April 1960, United Nations, *United Nations Treaty Series*, Vol. 508, p. 14. More recently, it was presented by Brazil to both Argentina and Paraguay at the IV Meeting of Chancellors of the Countries of the Plata Basin, in relation to water allocation in the Paraná River. In fact, the Brazilian Government adopted a theory developed by Sauser-Hall on the impossibility to divide the hydraulic power of water and the consequent necessity of a condominium. This idea appears in Article 2 of the Declaration of Asunción of 3 June 1971, which was emitted as a result of the Meeting of Chancellors. For the content of the Declaration, see COMIP (Comisión Mixta Argentino Paraguaya del Río Paraná), *Aprovechamiento energético del Río Paraná, Documentos y tratados* (Buenos Aires, 1992), pp. 78–79. For the alluded theory of the condominium, see Sauser-Hall, G., 'L'utilisation industrielle des fleuves internationaux', *Recueil des cours de l'Académie de droit international de la Haye*, Vol. 83 (1953-II), p. 488 et seq. See also Coret, A., *Le condominium* (Paris: Pedone, 1960).

63 Bouchez, supra, note 21, p. 790.

64 See Article 27 of this agreement in Parry, C., *Consolidated Treaty Series*, Vol. 116, p. 93.

65 *British and Foreign State Papers, 1815–1816*, Vol. 3, p. 720 (French text only). See also the Agreement concerning the maintenance, restoration and operation of the section of the Moselle common to the two States. Signed at Bonn on 14 September 1976 *in*, *United Nations Treaty Series*, Vol. 1045 (1977), pp. 285–287. Cf. Nolte, G., 'Moselle River', *in*, Bernhardt, R. (dir.), *Encyclopedia of Public International Law*, Vol. III (Amsterdam: North-Holland, 1997), p. 465.

66 The treaty has been in force since 20 February 1987. For an analysis of the regime of Lake Titicaca, see Querol, M., *Estudio sobre los convenios y acuerdos de cooperación entre los países de América Latina y el Caribe, en relación con sistemas hídricos y cuerpos de agua transfronterizos* (Santiago de Chile: CEPAL, 2003), pp. 37–42.

respectively, which runs adjacent to each coast. This area has an extension of two miles in the upper part of the river and of seven miles in the lower part. The rest of the waters of the river are waters of common use.[67]

A condominium is usually the result of an agreement between the states concerned. In *Land, Island and Maritime Frontier Dispute* (*El Salvador/Honduras: Nicaragua intervening*), the International Court of Justice stated that:

> [T]he historical examples of condominia, in the sense of arrangements for the common government of territory which would otherwise be, and in many cases already had been, delimited between two or more States, is ordinarily created by treaty. It is difficult to see how such a structured system of joint government could be created otherwise than by an agreement between the States concerned. It is true that condominium as a term of art in international law usually indicates just such a structured system for the joint exercise of sovereign governmental powers over a territory; a situation that might more aptly be called co-imperium.[68]

In the absence of an agreement, condominium could also be recognized as such by a judicial decision, as in the above-mentioned case.[69] At any rate, it is a legal notion, resulting from an international legal act. The fact that a certain territory—an international river or lake as far as we are concerned—is not delimited, does not necessarily entail that it is a condominium.

Co-sovereign states of a condominium are completely free to adopt whatever form of administration of their joint space they deem most suitable. In line with this idea, they could choose each to have their own administrative organs, or create a joint organ with international personality, instead, as in the case of many joint administrative commissions of international rivers and lakes. By way of example, and taking into account the examples of condominia discussed above, the Administrative Commission of the Rio de la Plata administers—by virtue of Article 13 of the Treaty of 1973—the shared waters of the

---

67 United Nations, *United Nations Treaty Series*, Vol. 1295, p. 294.

68 *Land, Island and Maritime Frontier Dispute* (*El Salvador/Honduras: Nicaragua intervening*), *Merits, Judgment, I.C.J. Reports 1992*, p. 351, at p. 597, para. 399.

69 The Court based its decision to recognize the existence of a condominium between El Salvador, Honduras and Nicaragua over the Gulf of Fonseca on the rules of state succession since there was no agreement on the matter. Ibid. For an analysis of the concept of condominium in this case, see Rossi, Ch. R., '*Jura Novit Curia?* Condominium in the Gulf of Fonseca and the "Local Ilusion" of a Pluri-State Bay', *Houston Journal of International Law*, Vol. 37(3) (2015), pp. 793–840.

river of the same name. Also, the International Moselle Company, initially set up in 1957 to finance the construction of the river's upgrade, manages the shipping charges and the operation and maintenance of the waterway, which are used for funding.

Although some voices view this method of delimitation (or non-delimitation, to be more precise) as outdated, it can be an attractive solution in more case than one, especially over disputed territories.[70] It has been put forward that at present states cannot afford to stop subjecting territory to their exclusive sovereignty. Giving up such exclusiveness would amount to a luxury according to this view.[71] Nevertheless, it could prove to be an adequate solution in cases of disputed freshwater resources. It is true, as we have already stated in our previous work on the subject,[72] that such a regime entails a perfect understanding between riparian states, an accordance that is not prevalent whenever there are opposing interests over the same watercourse. This can in turn present the condominium—or *co-imperium*—as a fragile institution.

Still, such a boundary would appear to be equitable and respectful of the rights of both riparian states over the watercourse in question. The equitable underlining of such a method of delimitation would therefore provide it with strength rather than weakness. So much so, that it has been lately considered as a possible solution to the pending conflict between Canada and Denmark over Hans Island, situated in the Kennedy Channel of Nares Strait, separating Ellesmere Island from Greenland.[73] Although this would be a case of condominium over a maritime island, it could also be a type of boundary preferred by states for international freshwater resources—they all amount to land boundaries after all—that have not yet been delimited or are the subject of disputing claims by neighbouring states. A condominium has also been postulated by Costa Rica to support its claim against Nicaragua before the ICJ in the case of *Certain Activities Carried Out by Nicaragua in the Border Area*.[74] Costa Rica

70 For an opposing view, see Samuels, J. H., 'Condominium Arrangements in International Practice: Reviving an Abandoned Concept of Boundary Dispute Resolution', *Michigan Journal of International Law*, Vol. 29 (2008), pp. 728–730.

71 "Qui plus est, ne pas pleinement exploiter et assujettir un cours d'eau-frontière à sa souveraineté est un luxe que les États concernés ne se permettent plus", states Caflisch. Supra, Caflisch, note 27, p. 18.

72 Querol, supra, note 17, p. 101.

73 Byers, M., *Who Owns the Arctic? Understanding Sovereignty Disputes in the North* (Vancouver: Douglas & McIntyre, 2010), p. 30. See also from the same author, *International Law and the Arctic* (Cambridge: Cambridge University Press, 2013), pp. 10–27.

74 *Certain Activities carried out by Nicaragua in the Border Area*, Application Instituting Proceedings Filed in the Registry of the Court on 18 November 2010, p. 8, paras. 11 and 12.

argued that the 1858 Treaty of Limits, delimiting the boundary between Costa Rica and Nicaragua from the Caribbean Sea to the Pacific Ocean, established a clear distinction between the boundary in the San Juan River and that of the Colorado River. In addition, pursuant to Article VI of the above-mentioned treaty, Nicaragua recovered possession of the port in 1861 and a condominium was established between both states over the Bay of San Juan.

Peculiar and exceptional as it may appear to be,[75] condominium is no less relevant nowadays. Neither does it lose any of its attractiveness as a fair and possible delimitation method for international rivers and lakes.

III *A Single Boundary at the Riverbank*

'La costa seca'—the dry shore—is the Spanish term used to make reference to those cases where the boundary lies on one of the riverbanks of a certain river or lake, leaving the whole freshwater course under the sovereignty of only one of the co-riparian states. Consequently, the other state ends up excluded from access to the international river or lake in question, at least in principle. It is indeed an eloquent term inasmuch as it accurately describes both the geomorphological features of such a boundary as well as the complete exclusion of the other co-riparian from enjoying sovereignty—and all the consequences this entails in terms of access, use and enjoyment over the watercourse in question.

Assuming that co-riparian states would not readily consent to be completely excluded from access to a frontier watercourse, it is indeed surprising that examples of this kind of boundary are still numerous.[76] As a matter of fact, it has even materialized at a national level, in watercourses separating federal states, as in the case of the Potomac River, between the state of Virginia and the District of Columbia, in the United States.[77]

Internationally, it is still possible to find watercourses delimited according to the 'single bank system' in every continent of the world. In Latin America, the Motagua and Tinto Rivers, between Guatemala and Honduras, are delimited

75 Verzijl, J. H. W., *International Law in Historical Perspective*, Vol. 6 (Springer, 1973), p. 69.

76 For an opposing view, see Bouchez, supra, note 21, p. 791 et seq. This author declares that such a method will only be applied when either one of the riparian states is much more powerful than the other and the first can press the latter politically to agree to such a boundary line, or as long as one of these states is not in the least interested in the river, which would be truly exceptional.

77 As a result of the adoption of this boundary line, the whole river lies within the territory of the District of Columbia. See *Virginia vs. District of Columbia*, 283 *U.S.* 348.

according to this method.[78] However, the most paradigmatic case in the region is that of the San Juan River, between Costa Rica and Nicaragua, mainly due to the various disagreements this type of boundary has created between the two states.[79] Article II of the Treaty of 15 April 1858 adopts the method of delimitation under study here, consequently leaving the whole San Juan River under Nicaraguan sovereignty.[80] By virtue of Article VI of the said agreement, Costa Rica was recognized as having "a perpetual right of free navigation" for certain purposes on the lower course of the river in question.[81]

The 'single bank system' has been adopted for many international rivers in Africa, such as the Senegal between Mauritania and Senegal.[82] It was also the thesis of Benin in its recent case against Niger before the International Court of Justice.[83] In Europe, France and Switzerland have adopted the single bank boundary line in the Foron,[84] the Morge, the Eau Noire and the Barberine,[85] among other cases.

78 Cf. the arbitration treaty of 16 July 1930 related to the territorial dispute between the two states, Martens, Ch. de, *Nouveau Recueil général des traités*, Vol. 31, p. 365 et seq.

79 For an in-depth study of the San Juan River, see Boeglin Naumovic, N., *La frontiére terrestre entre le Costa Rica et le Nicaragua*, Thèse pour le doctorat en droit de l'Université Panthéon-Assas (Paris II), Paris, 1996.

80 For the text of the treaty in its original Spanish version see República de Costa Rica, *Colección de tratados internacionales*, t. I (1892), pp. 97–101. An English version of the said treaty can be found in Parry, C., *Consolidated Treaty Series*, Vol. 118, pp. 439–443.

81 Ibid. Similarly, Argentina adopted this thesis in relation to the boundary of the River Plata immediately after the independence of Uruguay. Although in its early years the Banda Oriental—as Uruguay was called at that time—did not have any jurisdiction whatsoever over the said river, it enjoyed in fact numerous rights over it with the consent of Argentina. The treaty of 1973 made up for this by regulating the rights of both riparian states over the river in question. Cf. Barberis, J. & Pigretti, E., *Régimen jurídico del Río de la Plata* (Buenos Aires: Abeledo-Perrot, 1969), pp. 52–53.

82 Decree of 8 December 1933, *Journal Officiel de l'Afrique Occidentale Française* (1934), p. 69. This is also the existing boundary in a number of rivers, which divides Liberian territory from that belonging to the Ivory Coast. Declaration of 13 January 1911, Parry, C., *Consolidated Treaty Series*, Vol. 213, p. 2 et seq. Signed by Liberia and France, this declaration was later confirmed by the Ivory Coast after its independence in 1961. For a further analysis of this boundary, see Brownlie, I., *African Boundaries: A Legal and Diplomatic Encyclopedia* (London: The Royal Institute of International Law, 1979), p. 369 et seq.

83 *Frontier Dispute (Benin/Niger), Judgment, I.C.J. Reports 2005*, p. 90, at p. 99, para. 15.

84 Treaty of 16 March 1816, Parry, C., *Consolidated Treaty Series*, Vol. 65, p. 447 et seq.

85 Treaty of 10 June 1891, Parry, C., *Consolidated Treaty Series*, Vol. 175, p. 169 et seq. (for the Morge) and p. 173 et seq. (for the Eau Noire and the Barberine).

The option of the single bank boundary avoids the trouble of distributing competences amongst co-riparians by simply endowing one of them with the watercourse as a whole. Along this line, the Chamber of the Court called upon to solve the above-mentioned *Benin/Niger* case, acknowledged that such was the intention of the colonial French authorities from the correspondence suggesting that this method should be adopted as 'a clearer boundary' than the main navigable channel in the Niger River.[86] Similarly, the arbitral tribunal called upon to decide the *Guyana v. Suriname* case, concluded that

> The rationale for locating the border along the western bank of the Corentyne River rather than its thalweg and locating the border terminus on the western bank was to enable The Netherlands to exercise supervision of all traffic in the river.[87]

It has been postulated that such a boundary line is more easily recognizable on the ground.[88] However, this is not always the case in pratice. Indeed, the water level of the river in question will directly influence the boundary line: a high water mark will definitely favour the state under whose sovereignty the river is, whilst the excluded state would benefit more from a low water mark. Thus, it would become necessary to specify the meaning of the notion of riverbank to avoid future conflict between both riparian states.[89]

The intrinsic inequity underlying this type of boundary is manifest.[90] It is hard to understand why co-riparian states would willingly consent to being excluded from access and exploitation of a certain river or lake.[91] Unless, of

86 *Frontier Dispute (Benin/Niger)*, supra, note 83, p. 129, para. 85.

87 PCA, *Guyana v. Suriname*, Arbitral Award of 17 September 2007, p. 27, para. 137. (www.pca-cpa.org). Accessed on 20 April 2015.

88 Forteau, supra, note 55, p. 36.

89 The concept of bank is an "excellent example of the ambiguity of familiar terms". Jones, S. B., *Boundary-Making. A Handbook for Statesmen, Treaty Editors and Boundary Commissioners* (Washington: Carnegie Endowment for International Peace, 1945), p. 118. For a more in-depth study on the ambiguity and vagueness of natural language, see Querol, María, *The Concepts of Nullity and Sanction with Special Reference to the Law of Treaties*, Mémoire en vue de l'obtention du DES (Institut Universitaire de Hautes Études Internationales, Université de Genève, 2000), pp. 4–10.

90 Cf. supra, Boeglin Naumovic, N., 'De l'usage des cours d'eaux internationaux comme frontières', *in*, Boisson de Chazournes, L. & Salman, M. A. S. (eds.), *Water Resources and International Law* (The Hague: Hague Academy of International Law & Martinus Nijhoff, 2005), pp. 146–155.

91 Cf. Pondaven, supra, note 11, p. 68 et seq.

course, it were the result of a policy of force of one state over the other,[92] as occurred during colonial regimes.[93] In such cases, the boundary line would be more a circumstantial than an agreed one. In consonance with this idea, the Mirim Lagoon, between Brazil and Uruguay, was formerly delimited according to the single bank method. By virtue of the Treaty of San Ildefonso of 1 October 1777 between Spain and Portugal, the lagoon fell completely under Portuguese sovereignty.[94] With the access of both Brazil and Uruguay to independence, the two states concluded two treaties regarding their boundaries in 1851 and 1852 respectively.[95] Uruguay, however, was still excluded from access to the Mirim Lagoon and the Yaguaron River and denied the right to navigation. Later on, this situation was corrected by the Treaty of 30 October 1909, by virtue of which both states created a condominium over the waters of the Mirim Lagoon and the Yaguaron River.[96]

Most of the treaties stipulating the adoption of this method of delimitation for ex-colonies, were denounced at the time of decolonisation. Accordingly, new agreements were subscribed to, which resorted to other methods of delimitation contemplating the interests of both riparian states. In most cases,

92 Cf. Lapradelle, P. de, *La frontière* (Paris: Les Editions internationales, 1928), p. 95 et seq.

93 In fact, it was presented as a feasible boundary by many writers at the time. See among others Adami, who foresees its application in small lakes. Consequently, he provides the example of Lake Idro, between Austria and Italy, which followed the western bank of the lake itself, excluding Austria from access to the lake, *National Frontiers in relation to International Law* (London: Oxford University Press, 1927), p. 39 et seq.

94 Parry, C., *Consolidated Treaty Series*, Vol. 46, p. 361 et seq.

95 See the Treaties of 12 October 1851 (Parry, C., *Consolidated Treaty Series*, Vol. 106, p. 350 et seq.) and 15 May 1852 (Parry, C., *Consolidated Treaty Series*, Vol. 108, p. 139 et seq.). Article 1 of this latter agreement stipulates: "(...) From the embouchoure of the stream Chuy in the ocean, the line of division, shall ascend the said stream, and shall pass from thence, by the point of San Miguel, until it meets the lake Merim, and shall proceed along its western margin as far as the mouth of the Yaguaron (according to the *uti possidetis*)". For an analysis of this case, see Dipla, H., 'Le tracé de la limite sur les lacs internationaux', *Annuaire suisse de droit international*, Vol. XXXVI (1980), pp. 35–36. From the same author, see also 'Le tracé de la frontière sur les lacs internationaux', *in*, Zacklin, R., & Caflisch, L. (eds.), *The Legal Regime of International Rivers and Lakes* (The Hague: Martinus Nijhoff, 1981), pp. 247–306.

96 Martens, Ch. de, *Nouveau Recueil général des traités*, Vol. VI, p. 858 et seq.

the single riverbank has been replaced by the *thalweg* in the case of navigable rivers[97] and by the median line in lakes.[98]

While resorting to the single riverbank would appear to be progressively disappearing, those cases where it still exists have proved to be the source of continuing conflict among co-riparian states. So much so, that Costa Rica and Nicaragua have already submitted three cases to the International Court of Justice incidental to this type of boundary. Their disagreements with respect to this type of boundary and the interpretation of their respective rights under the 1858 Treaty of Limits regulating the boundary between them started as early as the 1980s.[99]

In the *Dispute regarding Navigational and Related Rights*, Costa Rica first resorted to the Court in order to ensure and specify the extent of its rights over the San Juan River, on the section running from a point three English miles below Castillo Viejo to the mouth of the river at the Caribbean Sea.[100] The Court acknowledged that the river belongs to Nicaragua, since—according to the Treaty of Limits of 1858, which is the law applicable to the matter—the border lies on the Costa Rican bank, with Costa Rica possessing a right of free navigation. However, the Parties differed both as to the legal basis of that right and, above all, as to its precise extent. The Court concluded that Costa Rica has the right of free navigation on the San Juan River for purposes of commerce. This right includes the transport of passengers and tourists.[101] Furthermore, the Court declared that Nicaragua has the power to regulate navigation on

97 Such is the case of the River Shatt-el-Arab, which was first delimited in 1847 by resort to the method of the riverbank (Treaty of Erzeroum, Parry, C., *Consolidated Treaty Series*, Vol. 101, p. 85 et seq.). This system was later combined with that of the *thalweg* of the river, in order to make up for the shortcomings of the first agreement (Treaty of 1937, League of Nations, *League of Nations Treaty Series*, Vol. 190, p. 241). Still, this latter treaty was denounced by Iran in 1969 and a new treaty was concluded in Algiers in 1975 taking into account the river's *thalweg* (Treaty of 6 March 1975, United Nations, *United Nations Treaty Series*, Vol. 1017, p. 55 et seq.).

98 Lake Titicaca was first delimited in accordance with the former administrative divisions at the time of the Spanish colonies. As a result, the Titicaca fell under Peruvian sovereignty, while the Vinamarca, which is connected to the former, corresponded to Bolivia. See the Treaty of 22 September 1829 *in*, Parry, C., *Consolidated Treaty Series*, Vol. 80, p. 97. Cf. Pondaven, supra, note 11, pp. 63–64.

99 Cf. *Costa Rica* v. *Nicaragua* and *Nicaragua* v. *Costa Rica* cases, *Judgment of 16 December 2015*, p. 33, para. 62 (www.icj-cij.org). Accessed on 16 December 2015.

100 *Dispute regarding Navigational and Related Rights* (*Costa Rica* v. *Nicaragua*), *Judgment, I.C.J. Reports 2009*, p. 213, at p. 230, para. 24.

101 Ibid., p. 269, para. 156.

the section of the San Juan River on which Costa Rica enjoys a right of free navigation. However, that power would not be unlimited. Indeed, a regulation must only subject the activity to certain rules, without rendering impossible, or substantially impeding, the exercise of the right of free navigation; it must be consistent with the terms of the treaty; it must have a legitimate purpose; it must not be discriminatory; and it must not be unreasonable.[102]

The next instance in which the Court was seized over the San Juan River, was the case concerning *Certain Activities carried out by Nicaragua in the Border Area (Costa Rica* v. *Nicaragua)*, filed by Costa Rica on 18 November 2010. In its application, Costa Rica alleged, in particular, that Nicaragua had invaded and occupied Costa Rican territory, and dug a channel thereon; it also reproached Nicaragua with conducting works (notably dredging of the San Juan River) in violation of its international obligations. A year later, on 22 December 2011, Nicaragua instituted proceedings against Costa Rica in a dispute concerning *Construction of a Road in Costa Rica along the San Juan River (Nicaragua* v. *Costa Rica)*. Nicaragua contended that Costa Rica was carrying out major road construction works in the border area between the two countries along the San Juan River, in violation of Nicaraguan sovereignty and several international obligations and with grave environmental consequences. On 17 April 2013, the Court decided by two separate orders to join the proceedings in the *Costa Rica* v. *Nicaragua* and *Nicaragua* v. *Costa Rica* cases.[103]

In its recent Judgment of 16 December 2015, the Court concluded that Costa Rica has sovereignty over the disputed territory and that by excavating three caños (channels) and establishing a military presence on Costa Rican territory, Nicaragua had violated Costa Rica's territorial sovereignty.[104] Also, by excavating two caños in 2013 and establishing a military presence in the disputed territory, Nicaragua breached the obligations incumbent upon it under the Order indicating Provisional Measures issued by the Court on 8 March 2011. In addition, the Court ruled that Nicaragua had breached Costa Rica's rights of navigation on the San Juan River pursuant to the 1858 Treaty of Limits. In turn,

102 Ibid., pp. 249–250, para. 87.

103 *Construction of a Road in Costa Rica along the San Juan River (Nicaragua* v. *Costa Rica), Joinder of Proceedings, Order of 17 April 2013, I.C.J. Reports 2013*, p. 184.

104 The Court recalled that the 'disputed territory' was defined by the Court in its Order of 8 March 2011 on provisional measures as "the northern part of Isla Portillos, that is to say, the area of wetland of some 3 square kilometres between the right bank of the disputed caño (dredged by Nicaragua in 2010), the right bank of the San Juan River up to its mouth at the Caribbean Sea and the Harbor Head Lagoon". Cf. *Certain Activities carried out by Nicaragua in the Border Area (Costa Rica* v. *Nicaragua), Provisional Measures, Order of 8 March 2011, I.C.J. Reports 2011*, p. 6, at p. 19, para. 55.

Costa Rica violated its obligation under general international law by failing to carry out an environmental impact assessment concerning the construction of Route 1856. All other submissions made by the parties were rejected.[105]

Apart from the above described conflict between Costa Rica and Nicaragua over the San Juan River, both Lake Tiberias and Lake Malawai are to this day the object of on-going unresolved disputes between Israel and Syria and Tanzania and Malawi respectively. The Armistice of 20 July 1949 between Israel and Syria establishes, only for military and not political purposes, a demarcation line between the two states.[106] In line with this idea, it adopts the boundary established in 1920 by France and Great Britain, the Mandatory Powers of Syria and Palestine respectively at the time of the agreement. This convention prescribed that the boundary should be the northern bank of Lake Tiberias, leaving the entire watercourse plus a territory of ten kilometres under Palestinian sovereignty.[107] Both the lake and the mentioned area are today considered by Israel to be Israeli territory, this argument being contested by Syria.[108]

Concerning Lake Malawi, the Anglo-German Treaty of 1890 first delimited Lake Malawi and divided the spheres of influence between Mozambique and Malawi.[109] This boundary was revised in 1954 by virtue of the Treaty of Lisbon between Great Britain and Portugal that established the median line.[110] Yet, with the access of the former Tanganyika—now Tanzania—to independence, the newly created state started, and has since been, claiming for recognition of its rights of access to the lake. It alleges that the lake should be delimited according to the median line, an argument which Malawi has continuously refused, claiming sovereignty over the portion of the lake that is not under the sovereignty of Mozambique. Consequently, Malawi claims its sovereignty over the whole portion of the lake that is contiguous to Tanzania, including the waters that are next to the shoreline of Tanzania. In 2012, Malawi referred the dispute to the African Union, when tensions arose as a result of Tanzania allegedly intimidating fishermen in the lake, which is potentially rich in oil and gas.[111] Malawi had awarded oil exploration licenses the previous year to

105 *Costa Rica* v. *Nicaragua* and *Nicaragua* v. *Costa Rica* cases, supra, note 99, pp. 76–77, para. 229.

106 Cf. Article II(2) of the said treaty, United Nations, *United Nations Treaty Series*, Vol. 42, p. 329 et seq.

107 League of Nations, *League of Nations Treaty Series*, Vol. 22, p. 365 et seq.

108 Cf. Dipla, supra, note 57, pp. 36–37.

109 Parry, C., *Consolidated Treaty Series*, Vol. 173, p. 271 et seq.

110 United Nations, *United Nations Treaty Series*, Vol. 325, p. 320 et seq.

111 http://www.bbc.com/news/world-africa-19978968. Accessed on 5 January 2016.

an English company, but Tanzania requested the company to postpone any planned drilling, without success. The conflict over Lake Malawi's boundary remains unsolved to this day. Thus, the method of the single riverbank offers more problems than solutions to co-riparian states.

IV *The Median Line*

Since as early as the sixteenth century, many adepts have advocated the use of the median line or *medium filum aquae* for international fresh watercourses, both for international rivers and international lakes.[112]

The median line is generally defined as "the line every point of which is equidistant from the nearest points on the shores of the two sovereignties".[113] It consists of a line made up of a series of points, all of which are equidistant to the nearest points of both opposite shores of the waterway in question.[114] It is the choice of treaty-makers and boundary commissioners in most cases of international lakes and in several cases of international rivers.[115]

As a matter of fact, as early as 22 October 1537, an arbitral award established the median line as the boundary in the Rhone River between the Swiss cantons of Bern and Valais.[116] Furthemore, the median line was implemented for the delimitation of the Bidassoa River, between France and Spain, by virtue of the Treaty of Bayonne in 1869.[117] More recently, in the *Frontier Dispute (Benin/Niger)*, the Special Chamber of the International Court of Justice called upon to resolve the dispute concluded that the boundary along the River Mekrou was the median line. In so doing, it argued that,

---

112 Among the authors who advocate in favour of the median line we can find Grotius, *De iure belli ac pacis*, 1672, libro 2, cap. 3, p. xviii. See also Puffendorf, *De iure naturae et gentium*, 1758, libro 4, cap. 7, p. xi and Vattel, *Le droit des gens ou principes de la loi naturelle*, 1758, livre I, chap. XXII, para. 266.

113 Boggs, W. S., *International Boundaries. A Study of Boundary Functions and* Problems (New York: Columbia University Press, 1940), p. 184. This definition has been taken up by almost every author who has written on the subject under analysis.

114 Cf. Schröter, F., supra, note 15, p. 957 et seq. Caflisch, supra, note 2, p. 69 et seq.

115 Among the doctrinal positions which claim in favour of the median line for the delimitation of international lakes, see Visscher, Ch. de, *Problèmes de confins en droit international public* (Paris: Pedone, 1969), p. 63 et seq. See also Boggs, W., supra, note 113, p. 184.

116 *Amtliche Sammlung der ältern Eidgenössischen Abschiede* (unter der Direction des eidgenössischen Archivars Jacob Raiser), Vol. 4, s. 1. c, (Lucern, 1878), pp. 884–886, especially p. 886 where it states: "beide Parteien (...) haben vereinbart (...) dass die Miete der Rhone zwischen beiden Parteien die March bilden soll".

117 Parry, C., *Consolidated Treaty Series*, Vol. 116, p. 85 et seq.

> [T]he Parties did not provide the Chamber with any documents that would enable the exact course of the thalweg of the Mekrou to be identified. The Chamber notes that in all likelihood there is a negligible difference between the course of the thalweg and the course of the median line of the River Mekrou, but considers that, in view of the circumstances, including the fact that the river is not navigable, a boundary following the median line of the Mekrou would more satisfactorily meet the requirement of legal security inherent in the determination of an international boundary.[118]

The Court applied this exact same reasoning to determine the median line as the boundary of the River Sirba in *Frontier Dispute* (*Burkina Faso/Niger*). In its *dictum* the Court stated:

> [T]he endpoint of the frontier line in the area of Bossébangou is located in the River Sirba. This endpoint is more specifically situated on the median line because, in a non-navigable river with the characteristics of the Sirba, that line best meets the requirements of legal security inherent in the determination of a boundary.[119]

As the Court stressed, among the virtues of this delimitation method would be the legal security it provides to co-riparian states. The median line would indeed profit from stability. What is more, it is more easily fixed than other systems herein analyzed since it can be fairly easily drawn on a large-scale map or recognized in a satellite photograph.[120] In turn, this would ensure an equitable solution to the riparian states.[121] Following the example of the application of the equidistance line in maritime delimitation, the median line would ensure,

---

118 *Frontier Dispute* (*Benin/Niger*), supra, note 83, p. 150, para. 144. The median line had also been adopted for the delimitation of the Niger River by the Treaty of 19 October 1906 between Niger and Benin, Martens, *Nouveau Recueil général des traités*, 3ème Série, Vol. 1, p. 612. However, a dispute arose between both states concerning the said boundary line. In the same case described above, the Chamber of the Court concluded that the boundary line in the Niger River was rather the *thalweg*, as will be further analyzed below.

119 *Frontier Dispute* (*Burkina Faso/Niger*), *Judgment of 16 April 2013, I.C.J. Reports 2013*, p. 44, at p. 85, para. 101. The Court was called upon to determine the course of the common frontier of Burkina Faso and Niger between the astronomic marker of Tong-Tong and the beginning of the Botou bend.

120 For an opposite view, see Schröter, supra, note 15, p. 959.

121 Cf. Pondaven, supra, note 11, p. 71 et seq.

at least in principle, certainty, equity and stability as integral parts of the process of delimitation.[122]

However, the application of the median line may reveal both technical and ethical difficulties. Technical shortcomings appear to be more evident in the case of lakes.[123] As a matter of fact, the geo-morphological configuration of certain lakes would render the application of the median line as such impossible in practice. An analysis of state practice in this respect shows that co-riparian states have tried to make up mostly for unstable banks by resorting to what Pondaven has classified as a conventional median line, as opposed to the geographical median line. As a result, there would be two types of median lines: the geographical one and the conventional one. The former offers no trouble insofar as it corresponds to the above-described definition of a line, which is equidistant to the respective opposite shores of the watercourse in question.[124] In turn, the conventional median line is made up of straight lines, which—in reality—correspond to the geographical median line. Following this classification, the case of Lake Geneva is usually described as that of a conventional median line.[125] By virtue of Articles 1 and 2 of the Treaty of 25 February 1953, the boundary in this lake consists of a median line on both ends of which there are two transversal lines, which connect the former with Hermance and St. Gingolph respectively.[126] This type of boundary line surmounts the shortcomings of lakes where there are islands or waters that are not very deep.[127]

---

122 Cf. *Guyana* v. *Suriname* case, supra, note 87, pp. 108–110, paras. 335–342, especially para. 341.

123 Cf. Schröter, supra, note 15, p. 916.

124 Pondaven, supra, note 11, p. 79 et seq.

125 *Revue générale de droit international public* (1960), p. 442 et seq. See also Schröter, F., supra, note 15, pp. 917–918.

126 See Villiger, M. E., 'Lake Geneva', *in, Encyclopedia of Public International Law*, published under the auspices of the Max Planck Institute for Comparative Public Law and International Law under the direction of Rudolf Bernhardt, Vol. 3 (1997), pp. 119–120. The Great Lakes of North America were similarly delimited by the Webster-Ashburton Treaty of 1842, Parry, C., *Consolidated Treaty Series*, Vol. 93, p. 415 et seq. Still, due to errors in the maps, a new treaty was negotiated later on by Canada and the United States and signed on 11 April 1908. The agreement in question entitles an international commission to draw the boundary, which is also a conventional median line. Actually, it consists of a line made up of a series of shorter straight lines that in reality correspond to the geographical median line of the lakes. For the text of the 1908 treaty, see Parry, C., *Consolidated Treaty Series*, Vol. 206, p. 377.

127 Cf. Jones, supra, note 89, p. 140.

On the contrary, the agreed boundary line for Lake Titicaca would amount to a paradigmatic example of the geographical median line. The Treaty of 15 February 1932 aims to revise the formerly adopted single bank method[128] through the application of the median line along the whole lake—i.e. as including both the Titicaca itself and Lake Vinamarca.[129]

An analysis of the conventional median line reveals that it amounts in reality to an agreed combination of the median line with other systems of delimitation, which is frequent in state practice. Therefore, one might well wonder whether the conventional median line is really a median line after all.

As regards flaws of both a technical and moral nature in international rivers, the complete disregard of the median line for the navigation interests of riparian states comes to light. Actually, adopting the median line could entail leaving the main channel of navigation totally under the sovereignty of only one of the riparian states. What would be worse, as Forteau accurately stresses, would be if the river in question was only navigable on one side of the median line or that the latter continuously cuts the main navigation channel, thus subjecting vessels on the channel to different sovereignties over very short fragments of the watercourse.[130] This point is especially relevant in the case of Latin American rivers. Unlike the case of European rivers ruled by freedom of navigation, a regional customary norm is applicable in Latin America by virtue of which navigation first must be consented to, unless otherwise agreed as in the case of the San Juan River between Costa Rica and Nicaragua, by the sovereign riparian states.[131] Such was actually the argument put forward by Niger before the International Court of Justice in support of the adoption of the *thalweg* for the River Niger.[132]

Finally, and also from an ethical standpoint, the application of the median line would merely attain primitive justice in the practice of watercourse

128 See supra, note 98.

129 Lake Moëro has also been delimited by resort to the geographical median line. On the contrary, this is not the case for Lake Tanganyka, despite what many authors have stated. See Schröter, F., supra, note 15, p. 917, fn. 59. The boundary of the latter consists of a combination of the median line and astronomical lines. Both boundaries were foreseen in the Declaration of 1885 of the Ministry of Foreign Affairs of the Independent State of Congo. Dipla, supra, note 95, pp. 29–31.

130 Forteau, supra, note 55, p. 37.

131 On the development of this customary rule at the regional level, see Barberis, J., 'Les règles spécifiques du droit international en Amérique Latine', *Recueil des cours de l'Académie de droit international de la Haye*, t. 235 (1992-IV), pp. 176–184.

132 *Frontier Dispute* (*Benin/Niger*), supra, note 83. See the Memorial of Niger, p. 132, para. 2.3.23 and its Reply, p. 140, para. 3.27.

delimitation in so far a it only divides the waters of a certain river or lake in two,[133] regardless of other elements to be taken into account, such as human considerations, which will be further examined below.

V *Der* Thalweg

The *thalweg* is a very popular system of river delimitation in state practice. So much so, that it has been and is still used for countless delimitations throughout the world,[134] especially in Latin America.[135]

Its popularity among delimitation methods is such that it has even been postulated as a rule of customary international law regarding boundary delimitation in navigable international rivers. Along this line, in the arbitration concerning the delimitation of its maritime boundary with Guyana, Suriname (*Guyana* v. *Suriname* case) contended that the *thalweg* of the river would amount to a special circumstance precluding the application of the

133 Gleditsch, K., 'Rivers as International Boundaries', *Acta Scandinavicae Iuris Gentium*, Vol. 21 (1952), p. 18.

134 In this regard, in Europe, the *thalweg* was implemented for the delimitation of the Meuse (Convention of 8 August 1843 between Belgium and the Netherlands, Parry, C., *Consolidated Treaty Series*, Vol. 95, p. 224 et seq.) and for the Rhine (Treaty of 6 July 1969 between Germany and France, United Nations, *United Nations Treaty Series*, Vol. 760, p. 305 et seq.). It is also present as the boundary for the African river, the Kagera between Tanzania and Rwanda (League of Nations, *League of Nations Treaty Series*, Vol. 190, p. 95 et seq.), as well as for the Australian river, the Fly (Treaty between Australia and Indonesia of 12 February 1973, United Nations, *United Nations Treaty Series*, Vol. 975, p. 3 et seq.). With regard to Asia, the Mekong (Convention of 25 August 1926 between French Indo-China and Siam, League of Nations, *League of Nations Treaty Series*, Vol. 69, p. 315 et seq.) can also be cited as an example of the application of such a delimitation system. In the Americas, see the case of the Río Grande (Treaty of 2 February 1848, Parry, C., *Consolidated Treaty Series*, Vol. 102, p. 29 et seq.) and the Oyapock, Kerindiotou, and Souarne Rivers (Exchange of Notes between Brazil and France (Guyana) of 18 July 1980, *Revue générale de droit international public*, Vol. 86 (1982), pp. 638–640).

135 Such is the case with the Paraná River. See Article 1 of the Treaty of 9 January 1872 between Paraguay and Brazil, Parry, C., *Consolidated Treaty Series*, Vol. 144, p. 155. See also the Treaty of 3 February 1876 between Argentina and Paraguay. Its Article 1 prescribes that the boundary divides the Paraguayan territory from the Argentinean by the middle current of the main channel of the Paraná River from its confluence with the Paraguay River, until it reaches the left bank of the limits of the Brazilian Empire ("por la mitad de la corriente del canal principal del río Paraná desde su confluencia con el río Paraguay, hasta encontrar por la margen izquierda los límites del Imperio del Brasil", Parry, C., *Consolidated Treaty Series*, Vol. 150, p. 248). The Uruguay River has also been delimited according to the *thalweg*. Cf. the Treaty of 3 February 1961 between Argentina and Uruguay, United Nations, *United Nations Treaty Series*, Vol. 635, p. 99 et seq.

equidistance principle, which is generally applicable in these cases.[136] In doing so, it invoked the commentary of the International Law Commission concerning the delimitation of the territorial sea, where it was said that the presence of a navigable channel could make a boundary based on equidistance inequitable and could indicate the appropriateness of utilizing the *thalweg* as the boundary line. Whilst recognizing the fact that navigational interests may constitute special circumstances, the arbitral tribunal dismissed the above-mentioned argument on the basis that it was not applicable. Rather, in that case, the *thalweg* was to the east of a line based on equidistance and where, indubitably, a binding agreement between the parties places the boundary in the river on the western bank.[137]

Contrary to this view, in the *Kasikili/Sedudu Island* (*Botswana/Namibia*) case the Court observed that:

> Treaties or conventions which define boundaries in watercourses nowadays usually refer to the thalweg as the boundary when the watercourse is navigable and to the median line between the two banks when it is not, although it cannot be said that practice has been fully consistent.[138]

As a matter of fact, an analysis of state practice shows that the *thalweg* has been adopted as the river boundary for both navigable and non-navigable waterways.

The first reference to the *thalweg* in the determination of a river boundary appears in Article 4 of the Peace Treaty of 27 October 1795 between Spain and the United States.[139] However, the term was first formally mentioned in the Peace Treaty of Lunéville of 9 February 1801 between France and the German Empire.[140] Since navigation was the main use of rivers at that time, the term

136 *Guyana v. Suriname* case, supra, note 87, p. 63, para. 226.

137 Ibid., pp. 94–95, para. 301.

138 *Kasikili/Sedudu Island (Botswana/Namibia), Judgment, I.C.J. Reports 1999 (II)*, p. 1045, at p. 1062, para. 24.

139 The said clause establishes that "the western boundary of the United States (…) is in the middle of the channel or bed of the River Mississipi", Parry, C., *Consolidated Treaty Series*, Vol. 53, p. 9.

140 Article 6 of the mentioned agreement determines "Le *thalweg* du Rin sera désormais la limite entre la République française et l'Empire germanique", Parry, C., *Consolidated Treaty Series*, Vol. 55, p. 479.

was mainly envisaged as a solution to the deficiencies of the median line in this regard.[141]

An etymological approach to this notion shows that the term derives from the German words 'das Tal', which means the valley, and 'der Weg', the way or the route to somewhere. Put together both terms are tantamount to the downstream route, or main channel.

It is worth highlighting that the *Dictionnaire de la terminologie du droit international* assigns various meanings to the notion in question:[142]

1) From a geographical point of view, it means the line of deepest soundings of a watercourse.
2) The middle of the riverbed. This is the first allusion made to the *thalweg* in diplomatic exchanges.
3) The middle of the river current or mid-channel.

Despite the number of treaties on river delimitation that have provided for the *thalweg*, most of them are inconsistent as to its exact meaning.[143] Actually, riparian states have adopted this system of delimitation in various and diverse senses. They amount to the following:

a) The most suitable way for downstream navigation at the lowest water level;[144]

141 Cf. de Lapradelle, who defines the thalweg as a "chemin variable suivi par les bateliers qui descendent le cours du fleuve frontière", supra, note 92, p. 202.

142 *Dictionnaire de la terminologie du droit international*, avec préface de Georges Basdevant (Paris: Sirey, 1960), pp. 601–603. See also Schultess, K., *Das internationale Wasserrecht*, Publikationen des Schweizer. Wasserwirstschafts-Verbandes No. 3 (Zurich, 1915), p. 12 et seq.

143 Cf. Jones, supra, note 89, p. 116.

144 The channel here defined forms a corridor, which becomes common to both riparian states. Caflisch believes that, in a certain way, it amounts to a natural boundary, for vessels would make use of the said channel due, precisely, to its natural conditions, supra, note 2, p. 73. Hence, the *thalweg* would amount to a boundary area. Some authors have pronounced themselves in favour of such a boundary. In this respect Bouchez emphasizes: "From the practical point of view the *thalweg* as a boundary area (...) is more desirable, as a ship in using the channel will never navigate without interruption on the one side of the boundary line. On the contrary, ships will nearly always navigate at the same time partly on the one side and partly on the other side of the precise boundary line", supra, note 21, pp. 793–794. Practice in this respect is more characteristic of an older time. It was adopted in the Peace Treties of 1919, more specifically in Article 30 of the Treaties of Versailles, Trianon, Saint-Germain, Neuilly and Sèvres, Martens, Ch. de, *Nouveau Recueil*

b) The line of continuous deepest soundings[145] (which corresponds to the geographical meaning mentioned above). By way of example, in the *Benin/Niger* case, the International Court of Justice concluded that the *thalweg* was the boundary line in the River Niger, understood as "the line of deepest soundings of the main navigable channel of that river";[146]
c) The line of continuous speed of water circulation;[147]
d) A combination of the above-mentioned meanings, i.e. the mid-channel or mid-current that usually coincides with the deepest part of the river, which is the way generally followed by boats sailing downstream.[148]

From all the different meanings we have presented, it can easily be concluded that the *thalweg* is both an ambiguous and vague term. Ambiguity and vagueness are inherent characteristics of natural language. While resorting to different uses—the descriptive or the directive one—both legislators and legal scientists (the latter including jurists and interpreters) employ natural language

---

des Traités, Vol. 11, p. 691 and Vol. 12, pp. 323, 423 and 664. See also Article 6 of the Peace Treaty of Lausanne, 25 July 1923, signed between Turkey and the Allies, League of Nations, *League of Nations Treaty Series*, Vol. 28, p. 11.

145 It is indeed a boundary line with all the inconveniences this entails for navigation. Article 2 of the Treaty of 5 April 1840 between France and the Grand Duchy of Baden adopts the *thalweg* in the above-described sense, Parry, C., *Consolidated Treaty Series*, Vol. 90, p. 31. The same meaning is specified with more detail in the Exchange of Notes of 15 March 1940, between Brazil and the United Kingdom in relation to British Guiana. It reads: "The *thalweg* is understood to imply the line of minimum level along the bed of the river throughout its length", United Nations, *United Nations Treaty Series*, Vol. 5, p. 71. Both Bouchez (supra, note 17, p. 793 et seq.), and Schröter (supra, note 15, p. 960, fn. 90), criticize the definition given by de Lapradelle, who states that the river boundary can be turned into a boundary line by taking into account the line made up of the deepest soundings at low water level of the river, supra, note 92, p. 203. The said authors argue that it is a very complicated solution given it is the case of a river with many depressions.

146 *Frontier Dispute (Benin/Niger)*, supra, note 83, p. 150, para. 146.

147 Such was the thesis of the Italian Government during the negotiation of the 28 Protocol of the European Commission for the Boundary Delimitation at the Danube between Bulgaria and Turkey, 21 October 1878–24 September 1879. Cf. Adami, *I confini di stato nella legislazione internazionale* (Roma: Stabilimento Poligrafico per l'Amministrazione della Guerra, 1912), p. 22. See also Boggs, supra, note 75, p. 184.

148 Cf. Institut de droit international, *Résolution de Heidelberg*, 1887, Article 3: "La frontière des Etats séparés par le fleuve est marquée par le thalweg, c'est-à-dire par la ligne médiane du chenal". Such is an artificial boundary line, which aims to combine the benefits of the median line and the *thalweg*. For this reason, it has been considered as the most modern and advanced solution in river delimitation. Cf. Caflisch, supra, note 2, p. 73.

for creating or describing legal norms.[149] This potential vagueness that characterises natural languages has been labelled 'the open texture of language'.[150] Both the legislator and the jurist can determine the scope of application and the special characteristics of the notions they resort to, consequently trying to remove as far as possible the intrinsic vagueness and ambiguity of such terms.[151] If the said notion has not been defined, both the interpreter and the jurist would be called upon to create for themselves the legal notions that assist them in the knowledge and systematic analysis of the legal order.[152] Agreements on river delimitation that resort to the *thalweg*—even if the notion under analysis has been defined—are not exempted from the above-described margin of lack of definition or blurriness. As a result, the issue becomes one of treaty interpretation.

The *Kasikili-Sedudu Island* case before the International Court of Justice may shed some light on this matter.[153] Placed in the Chobe River, the island in question lies some 20 kilometres (12.5 miles) upstream of Kazungula where the Chobe flows into the Zambezi. The island is referred to as 'Kasikili' by Namibia, while Botswana names it 'Sedudu'. Consequently, the parties requested the Court to establish the boundary around the island in the light of the Anglo-German Treaty of 1890,[154] which divided the respective spheres of influence of these states in Africa.

Accordingly, the Court observed that Article III(2) of the mentioned treaty determines the sphere of influence to be granted to Germany. As regards the dividing line when it reaches the Chobe River, the said article stipulates that it "descends the centre of the main channel of that river till its junction with the Zambezi, where it terminates". However, the German version of the agreement

149 Vernengo, R. J., 'About Some Formation Rules for Legal Languages', *in*, Engel, Salo (ed.), *Law, State and International Legal Order, Essays in Honor of Hans Kelsen* (Knoxville: The University of Tennessee Press, 1964), p. 340.

150 Cf. Carrió, G., *Notas sobre Derecho y Lenguaje* (Buenos Aires: Abeledo-Perrot, 1965), pp. 33–35. See also Hart, H. L. A., *The Concept of Law* (Second Edition, Oxford: Clarendon Press, 1994), pp. 121–132.

151 Cf. Barberis, J. A., 'Nouvelles questions concernant la personnalité juridique internationale', *Recueil des cours de l'Académie de droit international de la Haye*, Vol. 179 (1983-I), p. 160.

152 Cf. Eisenmann, Ch., 'Quelques problèmes de méthodologie des définitions et des classifications en science juridique', *Archives de philosophie du droit*, Vol. 11 (1966), pp. 26–29.

153 Supra, note 54, p. 3 et seq.

154 For the complete text of the treaty, see Parry, C., *Consolidated Treaty Series*, Vol. 173, p. 271 et seq.

in question alludes to the *Thalweg der Hauptalufes*.[155] Moreover, the 1890 Treaty did not provide any guideline as to where the main channel should be located. Hence, the Court had to interpret the term *thalweg* or main channel.[156] In doing so, the Court took into account that the "the natural features of a river may vary markedly along its course and from one case to another". Therefore, it considered the elements of width, depth and volume of the water and navigability as the necessary criteria for delimiting the scope of the term under discussion.

As a result of the application of these factors, the Court arrived at the conclusion that "in accordance with the ordinary meaning of the terms that appear in the pertinent provision of the 1890 Treaty, the northern channel of the River Chobe around Kasikili/Sedudu Island must be regarded as its main channel".[157] Similarly, in the *Bay of Bengal Maritime Boundary Arbitration between Bangladesh and India*, each party identified a different mid-stream of the main channel of the River Hariabhanga for the purpose of identifying the location of the land boundary terminus.[158]

Despite the above-mentioned *dictum* of the International Court of Justice in the *Kasikili/Sedudu Island* case, it is interesting to note that the Court has repeatedly decided otherwise in its more recent jurisprudence pertaining to fresh watercourse delimitation. As a matter of fact, both in the *Benin/Niger* and the *Burkina Faso/Niger* cases, the Court decided on the application of the

155 "(...) bis er den Tschobe-Fluss erreicht und setzt sich dann im Thalweg der Hauptlaufes dieses Flusses bis zu dessen Mündung in den Zambese fort, wo sie ihr Ende findet", ibid., p. 276.

156 It is interesting to stress that neither Namibia nor Botswana was party to the 1969 Vienna Convention on the Law of Treaties. Nonetheless, the International Court of Justice recognized, as it has done on previous occasions, that the rule contained in Article 31 of the said Convention is tantamount to a customary rule of international law, thus applicable to both state parties.

157 For a more in-depth study of the case, see Salman, S. M. A., 'International Rivers as Boundaries. The Dispute over Kasikili/Sedudu Island and the Decision of the International Court of Justice', *Water International*, Vol. 25(4) (2000), pp. 580–585. See also Ranjeva, R., 'Nouveaux aspects du droit des frontières en Afrique à la lumière de la jurisprudence de la Cour Internationale de Justice', *The International Legal System in Quest of Equity and Universality—Liber Amicorum Georges Abi*-Saab (The Hague: Martinus Nijhoff Publishers, 2001), p. 605 et seq.

158 PCA, *Bay of Bengal Maritime Boundary Arbitration between Bangladesh and India*), Arbitral Award of 7 July 2014, p. 42, para. 145. (www.pca-cpa.org). Accessed on 15 March 2015. See likewise, *Land and Maritime Boundary between Cameroon and Nigeria* (*Cameroon* v. *Nigeria: Equatorial Guinea intervening*), *Judgment, I.C.J. Reports 2002*, p. 303, at p. 425, para. 250 and p. 455.

median line as the boundary of an international watercourse based upon the fact that it was not navigable. Hence, one might well wonder whether the Court might be fostering the creation of a customary rule in this regard through a consistent and uniform practice in the case of non-navigable watercourses. Still, the existing different views as to the scope of the term under study as well as the need for interpreting its meaning on a case-by-case basis, prevents us, at present, from asserting that the *thalweg* consitutes a norm of customary international law, even for navigable waterways.[159]

All in all, as attractive as this method of delimitation might appear to be, it does possess its shortcomings if the aim sought is to ensure navigation in the river in question. In practice, a special agreement specifically regulating navigation would be needed. The case of the River Uruguay provides a good example in this regard. Whereas Articles 1 to 4 of the Treaty of 3 February 1961 between Argentina and Uruguay prescribe the adoption of the *thalweg* as the boundary line in the river, two separate treaty provisions specifically regulate the regime of navigation.[160] This was acknowledged by the International Court of Justice in the *Pulp Mills* case.[161]

In addition, the *thalweg* does not always assure equality of rights to the waters of the river in question to both riparian states, as it has been postulated. Natural alterations of a river such as variations of its course and movements of its sediments can turn the river boundary into a mere illusion. Therefore, it is crucial to take into account the natural configuration of a particular watercouse when resorting to this type of boundary—and actually to any type of boundary.

VI *Astronomical and Straight Lines*

Though seldom applied in the case of river boundaries, arbitrary straight lines would still be feasible in certain parts of very broad rivers. Whereas this method is much more popular with relation to boundaries in international lakes, such lines are more frequent in lakes situated in not too densely populated regions. Actually, their popularity in this latter case is owing mainly to geographical considerations. The impossibility of drawing a median line in the case of lakes with a rather quadrilateral shape calls for the application of straight lines to make up for this shortcoming. The system of straight lines has

159 Cf. Caflisch, supra, note 2, p. 74.

160 Cf. Articles 5 and 6 of the mentioned agreement. United Nations, *United Nations Treaty Series*, supra, p. 38, note 135.

161 *Pulp Mills on the River Uruguay (Argentina v. Uruguay), Judgment, I.C.J. Reports 2010*, p. 14, at p. 17, para. 26. (www.icj-cij.org). Accessed on 15 March 2015.

been applied in Latin America for the delimitation of various lakes between Argentina and Chile, such as Lake General Paz, Lake Buenos Aires, and Lake Pueyrredón.[162] Lake Guija, between Guatemala and El Salvador, has also been demarcated according to straight lines.[163] In this case, the boundary consists of a simple line that puts together short connecting lines with reference points of the territorial boundary. In this regard, it has been put forward that these boundaries would actually become an annex of the terrestrial boundary.[164]

Reference marks could also constitute a good solution for rivers that suffer from changes in their course. Taking into consideration islands in a particular watercourse might call for the application of straight lines, as well. Hence, straight lines would make up for the inconveniences of natural boundaries. The case of the River Uruguay illustrates this statement.[165] As a matter of fact—and as will be analyzed below—though the river is delimited by its *thalweg*, islands were taken into account during the stage of the negotiation of the relevant treaty. Hence, the river has two different boundary lines: one fixing the boundary for the river in question, and the other acting as a straight boundary line for the islands.

Astronomical lines, i.e. a watercourse delimitation with reference to parallels and meridians, is another possibility that states can resort to when agreeing to a certain boundary line for a particular river or lake. In this case, the boundary line would be formed by the succession of astronomical points put together. Particularly relevant for the delimitation of meandering rivers, or rivers with an unstable *thalweg*,[166] this method has been applied in a fraction

---

162 Paragraph 22 of the Report of the Mixed Commission charged with the implementation of the Arbitral Award of His British Majesty, King Edward VII on 20 November 1902 reads: "(...) hasta llegar a la orilla Norte del Lago General Paz (...) El límite cruzará entonces el Lago en su línea más corta (...)". Concerning Lake Buenos Aires, it states: "(...) el límite pasará en línea recta hasta la boca del más ancho canal del río Jeinemeni". Finally, as regards Lake Pueyrredón, it is prescribed that "De esta junta cruzará el Lago pasando directamente hasta un punto en la cumbre de la colina (...)", Oficina de límites internacionales, *La frontera argentino-chilena. Demarcación general 1894–1906*, t. 1, (Buenos Aires, 1908), pp. 360–363.

163 Treaty of 9 April 1938, which declares: "atravesando el lago de Guija en línea recta hasta el punto más septentrional de la península llamada Tipa Afuera (...)", League of Nations, *League of Nations Treaty Series*, Vol. 189, p. 275.

164 Pondaven, supra, note 11, p. 95. However, this has been contested by Dipla, supra, note 95, p. 44.

165 Supra, p. 28, note 97.

166 Cf. Schröter, supra, note 15, p. 964.

of the River Kagera, between Tanzania and Rwanda,[167] and in North America for the delimitation of the Saint John River.[168]

Furthermore, astronomical lines have been applied in the delimitation of lakes that constitute the meeting point of many states.[169] This is the case of Lake Victoria, which is shared by Uganda, Kenya and Tanzania. After the independence of these riparian states, they decided to take up the boundary just as it had been established at the time of the Anglo-German Treaty of 1890. This agreement foresees in its Article 1 the tracing of the boundary according to astronomical orientation.[170] However, the presence of islands on the eastern part of the lake also had to be taken into account. Thus, it became necessary to resort to another method of delimitation, which would take into consideration the exact location of the islands. The three riparian states decided to adopt the delimitation method that had been formerly used by Great Britain at the time when Kenya was half colony, half British protectorate. By virtue of an Order-in-Council of 1926, Great Britain stipulated that the boundary in this part of the lake should be made up of a series of short straight lines that would avoid cutting the islands that are situated between Kenya and Uganda on the one hand, and between Kenya and Tanzania on the other.[171]

The above-analyzed example brings to light the flaws of astronomical lines with regard to the presence of islands in watercourses. Also, in the case of international rivers, the application of these lines may result in the exclusion of co-riparian states from access to the main navigable channel of the river in question. The disregard of such lines for navigational interests is thus also exposed. Whilst they would be especially applicable in meandering rivers, this would not be the case when the particular watercourse is overly sinuous. The

167 Article 2 of the Treaty between Great Britain and Belgium of 22 November 1934, League of Nations, *League of Nations Treaty Series*, Vol. 190, p. 95 et seq.

168 Formerly delimited by resort to the *thalweg*, the unstableness of this latter in a part of the river made it necessary to redefine the boundary line by means of astronomical lines. In this respect, see the Webster-Ashburton Treaty of 1824. See also Jones, supra, note 89, p. 112 and the drawing he presents at page 117 (figure 15).

169 Cf. Schröter, supra, note 15, p. 920.

170 With relation to the sphere of influence to be granted to Germany in East Africa, Article 1 of the treaty in question reads: "(…) (the line) thence is drawn direct to the point on the eastern side of Lake Victoria Nyanza, which is intersected by the 1st parallel of south latitude; thence crossing the lake on that parallel, it follows the parallel to the frontier of the Congo Free State, where it terminates", Parry, C., *Consolidated Treaty Series*, Vol. 173, p. 273.

171 Cf. Dipla, supra, note 95, pp. 25–26. See also McEwen, A. C., *International Boundaries of East* Africa (Oxford: Clarendon Press, 1971), p. 299 et seq.

number of short lines aiming to get over the sinuosity might end up in a very difficult construct, which would run counter to the aim of simplicity that the treaty makers or boundary commissioners might have sought to achieve.

Nevertheless, riparian states are always free to combine astronomical lines with any other line they may consider suitable, given the configuration of the river or lake in question. The boundary line is usually integrated with reference to both parallels and meridians and straight lines or with reference to one of the other systems of delimitation examined above. Above all, astronomical and geometrical lines are tantamount to unchanging lines, which makes them fairly easy to determine and mark with precision, thus offering security and stability to co-riparian states.[172]

This latter type of boundary line—made up of both astronomical and straight lines—was addressed by the International Court of Justice in its decision in *Land and Maritime Boundary between Cameroon and Nigeria* (*Cameroon v. Nigeria: Equatorial Guinea intervening*) in the area of Lake Chad where these states are co-riparian. On the one side, Nigeria argued that Lake Chad had never been subject to any form of delimitation due to two main reasons: first, the imprecision as to the longitude of one of the astronomical references taken into account to draw the line; and second, the blurred meaning of the words 'mouth of the Ebeji' in the light of both the changes in the course of the river as well as the shrinking dimensions of the lake.[173] Cameroon, on the other side, stated that the boundary line was made up of the combination of astronomical references and a straight line to the mouth of the Ebeji River.[174] The Court concluded in favour of Cameroon's claim, declaring that the boundary line had in fact been established by different agreements and later declarations by the mandatory powers at the time of the states' respective colonial regimes, consisting of astonomical and straight lines.[175]

The combination of astronomical and straight lines still does not solve the problem of existing islands in the watercourse in question. The case of Lake Chad is particularly illustrative in this respect. Bordered by Cameroon, Chad,

172 Gleditsch, supra, note 133, p. 21.

173 See, in particular, paras. 45 and 51 of the judgment. Supra, note 158.

174 Moreover, such boundary had been further specified in the Milner-Simon Declaration of 1919 and the Thomson-Marchand Declaration of 1929–1930 as incorporated in the 1931 Henderson-Fleuriau Exchange of Notes. See especially para. 47 of the judgment (ibid.).

175 The Court "decides that the boundary between the Republic of Cameroon and the Federal Republic of Nigeria in the Lake Chad is delimited by the Thomson-Marchand Declaration of 1929–30, as incorporated in the Henderson-Fleuriau Exchange of Notes of 1931", para. 325 of the judgment. See also paras. 49–50 of the same instrument (ibid.).

Niger and Nigeria, Lake Chad was delimited at the time when these states were former colonies.[176] The boundaries of Lake Chad were agreed by a series of Anglo-German, Anglo-French, and Franco-German agreements respectively.[177] The strategic interest of the lake for the above-mentioned colonial powers was particularly evident during the nineteenth century. In the area that divides Chad from Niger, a former agreement on French administrative divisions—by virtue of the *uti possidetis*—was applied.[178] As a result, Lake Chad was delimited by both astronomical and straight lines, some of which cut certain islands in the sector that divides Chad from Nigeria, in the Bogomeron Archipelago.

VII *Combination of Various Delimitation Systems*

Taking due regard of the natural configuration of an international watercourse on the one hand, and of the uses sought after by the co-riparian states on the other, delimitation is not always easy in practice. The different methods of delimitation examined all have their shortcomings when only one of these systems is exclusively applied as the boundary line in certain rivers and lakes. All in all, states remain free to combine the methods that would best adjust to their needs. All the methods of fresh watercourse delimitation that we have presented so far depend fully on the choice and consent of the states, after all.

Along this line, the Treaty of the Río de la Plata of 19 November 1973 has succeeded in reconciling both the geo-morphological features of the river and

176 For a study of this lake, see Sand, P. H., 'Lake Chad', *in*, *Encyclopedia of Public International Law*, published under the auspices of the Max Planck Institute for Comparative Public Law and International Law under the direction of Rudolf Bernhardt, Vol. 3 (1997), pp. 113–116.

177 Among the treaties between Germany and Great Britain concerning the lake, see those of 15 November 1893 (Martens, Ch. de, *Nouveau Recueil des Traités*, Vol. 20, p. 276 et seq.), and 19 March 1906 (Martens, Ch. de, *Nouveau Recueil des Traités*, Vol. 2, p. 391 et seq.). In relation to the treaties signed by France and Germany, see, in particular, that of 15 March 1898 (Martens, Ch. de, *Nouveau Recueil des Traités*, Vol. 29, p. 116 et seq.), that of 18 April 1908 (Martens, Ch. de, *Nouveau Recueil des Traités*, Vol. 1, p. 612 et seq.), and that of 4 November 1911 (Martens, Ch. de, *Nouveau Recueil des Traités*, Vol. 5, p. 651 et seq.). The Versailles Peace Treaty rejected this agreement. Finally, as regards the Anglo-French treaties, see, in particular, those of 14 June 1898 (Martens, Ch. de, *Nouveau Recueil des Traités*, Vol. 29, p. 116 et seq.), which was replaced by those of 8 April 1904 (Martens, Ch. de, *Nouveau Recueil des Traités*, Vol. 35, p. 352 et seq.), and 29 May 1906 (Martens, Ch. de, *Nouveau Recueil des Traités*, Vol. 35, p. 463 et seq.). It is worth mentioning also the Exchange of Notes of 9 January 1931 (Martens, Ch. de, *Nouveau Recueil des Traités*, Vol. 25, p. 478 et seq.).

178 Cf. Sand, supra, note 176, p. 114.

the main interests of each riparian state in a truly innovative way.[179] Indeed, its originality makes it more than a boundary agreement: it is a real statute for the river.[180] The treaty establishes different boundaries for the waters of the river on the one hand, and for the riverbed, subsoil and islands, on the other hand. Concerning the former, Article 2 of the said agreement stipulates that each riparian state will have a zone of seven sea miles of exclusive jurisdiction along each riverbank, which will narrow up to two sea miles at the upper part of the river.[181] The remaining middle waters—regulated in Article 3 onwards—are tantamount to a *condominium*, as explained above. With relation to the riverbed and subsoil, these are delimited by a boundary line, which is made by resorting to astronomical references.[182] There are therefore three different methods of delimitation foreseen in this agreement, each of which intends to maximize as much as possible the natural configuration of the Río de la Plata with the uses envisaged by its co-riparian states.

There are indeed numerous boundary agreements in which states have not contented themselves with only one method of delimitation. Arbitral and judicial decisions usually prescribe the application of several delimitation methods in boundary disputes involving international watercourses. This is especially true—and insofar as the norms applicable to the case so allow—in those cases where the application of one single method would result in an inequitable solution to both co-riparians or would not suffice to take due account of the presence of islands in the river or lake in question. The *Benin/Niger* case, analyzed in this monograph, is illustrative in this respect. Whilst the Court recognizes that the boundary in the River Niger is the *thalweg*, it concludes that the boundary departs from this line in the section of the river where there are islands, to go back to the *thalweg* in the remaining section of the said watercourse.[183]

179 *International Legal Materials*, Vol. XIII (1974), p. 251 et seq. For an analysis of this treaty, see Barberis & Pigretti, supra, note 81. See also Gros Espiell, H., 'Le traité relatif au Rio de la Plata et la façade maritime', *Annuaire français de droit international*, Vol. 21 (1975), pp. 241–249 and Armas Barea, C. A., 'El tratado del Río de la Plata y su Frente Marítimo', *Revista de derecho internacional y ciencias diplomáticas*, Vol. 25 (1973/74), pp. 7–31. More recently, Del Castillo-Laborde, L., *The Rio de la Plata and Its Maritime Front Regime* (Leiden: Martinus Nijhoff, 2008), 428 p.

180 Cf. Armas Pfirter, F.; Barberis, J. A.; Béraud, A. & Freyre, N., 'Límites de la República Argentina', *Cuadernos de Derecho Internacional*, Vol. 2 (Buenos Aires: Ábaco-Depalma, 2000), pp. 128–143.

181 Cf. Article 2 of the mentioned treaty.

182 Cf. Article 41 of the 1973 Treaty. This line is also the boundary for the islands of the river.

183 *Frontier Dispute (Benin/Niger)*, supra, note 83, p. 151, para. 146.

The choice to combine more than one system of delimitation in an international watercourse could have its cause in the desire to render compatible the opposing uses of the river by riparian states. Cooperation among riparian states might lead them in the short run to apply a combination of these systems more often. As in the case of *condominium*, combining different methods of delimitation could even provide a good solution for numerous international watercourses that are still disputed by their riparian states. In line with this view, it is worth noticing that almost every international lake possesses a boundary which has been conventionally established, the cases of the Caspian Sea and Lake Constance being exceptions to the rule.[184] On the basis of either geographical or historical circumstances, riparian states of both of the lakes mentioned above have been unable till the present to reach an agreement as regards the boundary for those watercourses.

Resorting to such combinations of various and diverse segments of boundary line would provide co-riparians with a compromise solution to long-term disputes over many watercourses, which still, at present, remain unresolved. Certainly, such was the case in the Río de la Plata examined above. The co-riparian states involved came to the conclusion that sticking to the claim of applying one single boundary delimitation method to the river would only prolong an unresolved dispute where there were surely no winners. Instead, negotiating and further agreeing on the combination of different delimitation systems in the river in question provided them with an original solution in which they could all profit from the uses of the river and take into account the majority of the particularities of the river's physical composition.

184 For an analysis of the situation of the Caspian Sea, see Janusz-Pawletta, B., *The Legal Status of the Caspian Sea: Current Challenges and Prospects for Future Development* (Berlin: Springer, 2015), 176 p. See also Griffiths, D. N., 'What's in a Name: Take the Legal Regime in the Caspian Sea (or Lake)', *Ocean Yearbook*, Vol. 23 (2009), pp. 161–192 and Sadigov, Z., 'Legal Issues of the Status and Territorial Division of the Caspian Sea', *The Journal of International Maritime Law*, Vol. 11 (2005), pp. 372–375. With regard to Lake Constance, see Blatter, J., 'Lessons From Lake Constance: Ideas, Institutions and Advocacy Coalitions', *in*, *Reflections on Water: New Approaches to Transboundary Conflicts and Cooperation* (Cambridge, MA: MIT Press, 2001), pp. 89–122. Schlag, M., 'Die österreichische Bundesgrenze auf dem Bodensee', *Austrian Journal of Public International Law*, Vol. 43 (1992), pp. 241–266. See also Frowein, J. A., 'Lake Constance', *in*, *Encyclopedia of Public International Law*, published under the auspices of the Max Planck Institute for Comparative Public Law and International Law under the direction of Rudolf Bernhardt, Vol. 3 (1997), pp. 116–119.

Part 2: Variations in an International River Boundary

I *Natural Alterations in an International River*

It is nowadays uncontested that land boundaries benefit from legal stability. Indeed, once a boundary has been agreed upon by neighbouring states, according to international law such a boundary line will remain unaltered unless the said states otherwise consent. However, international rivers and lakes amount to natural geographical features. Whilst established as international boundaries between states by virtue of a conventional legal norm, they are still based on natural elements. As a result, they are subject to the inclemencies of nature and their inherent unpredictability.[185] Thus, the inevitable query is whether those boundaries partake in the above mentioned stability, especially when their immobility cannot be assured.

In as far as they consist of natural accidents, the configuration of an international river is contingent on change. This change can happen naturally or as a result of human activity in the river. Undoubtably, both natural causes and human intervention may affect the geophysical structure of a river and it is certainly interesting to examine the legal consequences of such alterations.

With regards to natural alterations in a river, they are fairly easily recognizable by the human eye when they occur abruptly, or suddenly, as in the case of a natural disaster. But there are other changes, assessment of which can solely be achieved through technical means, as they take place extremely slowly.

At present, the international legal order does not provide any apposite answer with regards to modifications in a river as a result of natural causes. The absence of general rules prescribing the legal consequences of such variations require a case-by-case approach to an eventual solution. All in all, it is currently generally understood that international agreements on river boundaries do provide for, if not explicitly at least tacitly, the natural alterations from which the watercourse in question might suffer. In so doing, they might foresee the combination of more than one method of delimitation, as discussed above, especially astronomical lines combined with one or more of the other methods that exist.[186]

1 Changes in the Course and in the Riverbed

The geo-morphological and hydrological configuration of a river can well condition its probability of being subjected to changes in both its course and its riverbed. It has been suggested that the particular features of certain rivers

185 Cf. Caflisch, supra, note 2, p. 80.
186 Barberis, supra, note 3, p. 101.

make them more susceptible than other rivers to natural alterations.[187] There are three different types of rivers, in this respect. First of all, there are rivers which flow in narrow valleys. The channel of these rivers is usually cut down actively, thus decreasing the probability of changing their course. Then, there are rivers or parts of rivers that build up their beds actively due to the large quantity of sediments they carry. Generally, this kind of river changes its main channel rather frequently. Finally, the 'average rivers', may turn out to be extremely meandering. This may cause, more often than not, some lateral shift in the course of the river.

The above-mentioned changes may happen either slowly or in an abrupt and sudden manner. Material sediments flowing downstream in a particular river may well sluggishly deposit themselves on one of the riverbanks or on the riverbed. This phenomenon is better known as accretion or *alluvio*. On the contrary, avulsion (*avulsio*) is characterized by its abruptness. Such a sudden alteration may have its cause in either a geological phenomenon or in a natural disaster such as an extraordinary flood.[188] Do these changes affect the boundary line—and in which case how? Can a change in the course of a river or in its riverbed consequently shift the boundary of a river between two or more states? If so, the legal consequences of such an alteration in terms of territorial sovereignty and access to the watercourse could be decisive for one or both co-riparian states and, as such, need to be analyzed.[189]

Once again, in the absence of general rules foreseeing the legal consequences of such alterations, state practice comes up with the most diverse solutions to the matter.[190] Riparian states may agree that, whilst the boundary will remain unaltered in the case of avulsion, it will follow the watercourse along its new bed in the event of an accretion. In other words, whilst a progressive change taking place over time would affect territorial sovereignty among the co-riparians, a swift modification would not consequently encompass a change in title. Actually, such solution finds its direct antecedent in the classic

187 Boggs, supra, note 113, pp. 119–120.

188 Barberis, J. A., 'Un precedente poco conocido sobre la aplicación del uti possidetis a un río limítrofe que cambia de curso', *Anuario de Derecho Internacional* (Universidad de Navarra), Vol. x (1994), p. 78.

189 Pellet states that, whilst the boundary line based upon the *thalweg* is more sensitive to accretion, the single bank system would 'resist' it better, inasmuch as the respective positions and rights of the co-riparian states remain unaltered in case of change. On the contrary, the single bank method could render a 'particularly extravagant situation' in case of avulsion. Pellet, A., 'Les problèmes posés par l'alluvionnement', *in*, Aurescu, B. & Pellet, A. (eds.), *Actualité du droit des fleuves internationaux* (Paris: Pedone, 2010), p. 56.

190 Concerning state practice, see Dipla, supra, note 95, p. 612 et seq.

scholars of international law, who applied the rules of private Roman law in order to regulate this kind of situation.

The *Chamizal* case, between Mexico and the United States, is emblematic in this respect.[191] The boundaries between both states at the Rio Grande and Colorado River are regulated by Articles v and vi of the Guadalupe-Hidalgo Treaty of 2 February 1848, which happens also to be the oldest treaty still in force between Mexico and the United States.[192] The said agreement—also known as the Treaty of Peace, Friendship, Limits and Settlement—put an end to the Mexican-American War (1846–1848). By virtue of this treaty, the Rio Grande was established as an international boundary between both states, thus granting the United States territorial sovereignty over California and a large area comprising roughly half of New Mexico, most of Arizona, Nevada, Utah, and parts of Wyoming and Colorado. With regards to the Rio Grande, Article v of the treaty stipulates:

> The boundary line between the two Republics shall commence in the Gulf of Mexico, three leagues from land, opposite the mouth of the Rio Grande, otherwise called Rio Bravo del Norte, or opposite the mouth of its deepest branch, if it should have more than one branch emptying directly into the sea; from thence up the middle of that river, following the deepest channel, where it has more than one, to the point where it strikes the southern boundary of New Mexico; thence, westwardly, along the whole southern boundary of New Mexico (which runs north of the town called Paso) to its western termination; thence, northward, along the western line of New Mexico, until it intersects the first branch of the river Gila; (or if it should not intersect any branch of that river, then to the point on the said line nearest to such branch, and thence in a direct line to the same); thence down the middle of the said branch and of the said river, until it empties into the Rio Colorado; thence across the Rio Colorado, following the division line between Upper and Lower California, to the Pacific Ocean.[193]

191 *Chamizal Case*, Arbitral Award of 5 June 1911, *Reports of International Arbitral Awards*, Vol. xi, pp. 309–347. For a study of this case, see Anzilotti, D., 'Intorno agli effetti delle modificazioni del corso di un fiume sul confine fra due Stati', *Rivista di Diritto Internazionale* (1914), pp. 73–83.

192 Parry, C., *Consolidated Treaty Series*, Vol. 102, p. 29 et seq.

193 (https://www.ourdocuments.gov/doc.php?doc=26&page=transcript). Accessed on 21 May 2016.

Between the period that ran from 1854 until 1861 and the years 1864 and 1911 the Rio Grande suffered a shift of its riverbed to the south due to natural causes, causing the formation of the area of the Chamizal.[194] What is really interesting in this case is that the river in question was subjected to both types of natural alterations: *alluvio* and *avulsio*. Whilst the movement was gradual and progressive in the first period, it was abrupt in the last period. Confronted with this natural change, both co-riparian states digressed in their interpretation of the terms of the Guadalupe-Hidalgo Treaty and adopted opposite positions. On one side, Mexico contended that the Chamizal tract having been formed before the coming into force of the convention of 1884, the said treaty could not be applied retroactively. It further argued that, even assuming the case to be governed by the terms of the Treaty of 1884, the changes in the channel of the river amounted to an avulsion, which did not in the least affect the actual international boundary. On the other side, the United States alleged that it was indeed a case of accretion, which consequently altered the river boundary as such. The Mixed Commission entrusted by the states in question to resolve the dispute, took into account both periods described and adjudicated, granting to the United States the portion of territory that was formed as a result of the first shift of the river, and to Mexico the one corresponding to the last movement of the river.[195]

It is worth noticing that in the *Chamizal* case, Article V of the treaty under discussion stipulates:

> The boundary line established by this article shall be religiously respected by each of the two republics, and no change shall ever be made therein, except by the express and free consent of both nations, lawfully given by the General Government of each, in conformity with its own constitution.

194 Article 1 of the agreement concluded on 24 June 1910 between the two states to submit the case to arbitration stipulates that: "The Chamizal tract in dispute is located at El Paso, Texas, and Ciudad Juarez, Chihuahua, and is bounded westerly and southerly by the middle of the present channel of the Rio Grande, otherwise called Rio Bravo del Norte, easterly by the middle of the abandoned channel of 1901, and northerly by the middle of the channel of the river as surveyed by Emory and Salazar in 1852 (...)". Supra, note 191, p. 313.

195 The United States refused to enforce the award and the question remained unsolved for many years. It was only in 1963 that both co-riparian states could settle their differences and signed a new treaty foreseeing the setting-in-motion of certain works in order to move the watercourse to its former riverbed.

Co-riparian states may prefer to adopt an even more precise wording in their agreement and establish that the international boundary will follow any possible movement of the international watercourse. Actually, this is the solution envisaged in the Final Protocol of the Boundary Commission between Syria and Turkey, of 3 May 1930. This agreement prescribes that the boundary for both rivers will always be their respective *thalweg*, regardless of any change whatsoever that may occur in either its bed or its course.[196]

In addition, it can be agreed that the river boundary will remain unaltered regardless of any possible change—either abrupt or slow and gradual—in the river's course. Such is the case of the Boundary Treaty of 7 April 1961 for the River Uruguay, whose Article 3 foresees:

> The demarcation agreed upon in the preceding articles shall be that consistent with the general condition of the river on the date on which this Treaty was signed.
>
> The agreed boundary shall be permanent and unalterable and shall not, except as provided for in article 1, paragraph (A), be affected by any natural or artificial changes which the features that now determine the boundary may undergo in the future.[197]

Notwithstanding the apparent absence of an international customary norm regulating the application of different solutions in the cases of accretion and avulsion respectively, the International Court of Justice implied its existence in the *Land, Island and Maritime Frontier Dispute* between El Salvador and

196 See also the Exchange of Notes of 27 October and 1 November 1932 between Great Britain and Brazil over the Mahu and Tucutu Rivers in British Guiana, League of Nations, *League of Nations Treaty Series*, Vol. 177, pp. 128–133. Another example of the same solution is the Boundary Convention of 8 August 1843, between Belgium and the Netherlands. Paragraph 1 of Article 11 of the said treaty reads: "Si, par un catastrophe quelconque, la Meuse vient à abandonner son lit actuel et à s'en creuser un nouveau, le thalweg de ce nouveau lit n'en continuera pas moins à former limite entre les 2 Etats", Parry, C., *Consolidated Treaty Series*, Vol. 95, p. 229.

197 United Nations, *United Nations Treaty Series*, Vol. 635, p. 104. This solution also has been applied to national rivers that are tantamount to boundaries between federal units of a state. This is the case of the Desaguadero River between Mendoza and San Luis, in Argentina. Faced with a shift of the course of the river, the Inter-provincial Commission competent to decide the legal consequences of such a change applied the principle of *uti possidetis* on which the states had previously agreed. For an analysis of this example, see Barberis, supra, note 3, pp. 61–82.

Honduras.[198] However, this would not suffice in itself to create such a general rule of international law.

In the *Benin/Niger* case, Benin maintained that the River Niger is subject to siltation, which had led to a change in its course over time affecting in particular the right bank. It further claimed that the said siltation, together with the formation of virtually permanent sandbanks, had allegedly resulted in a change in the position of the main navigable channel around the islands. It specifically referred to the islands of Kotcha Barou, Gagno Goungou and Dolé Barou. Whilst acknowledging the existence of this phenomenon, Niger contended that, because of the nature of the rocks in the stretch of river concerned, there had been no significant change in the course of the main channel for more than a century, and that there was no substantial difference in the configuration of each bank.[199] The Special Chamber of the Court deciding the case observed that the position of the main navigable channel as determined by each of the missions was very similar. This would indicate that the riverbed was relatively stable and that any siltation which has taken place has rarely led to a noticeable change in the location of the main navigable channel.[200]

In *Territorial and Maritime Dispute between Nicaragua and Honduras in the Caribbean Sea*, Nicaragua recalled that the terminus of the land boundary between Nicaragua and Honduras was established by the 1906 Arbitral Award at the mouth of the principal arm of the River Coco. However, since 1962, the mouth of the River Coco had moved more than one mile north and east due

198 Supra, note 68, p. 546, para. 308, in which the Court asserts: "The contention of El Salvador that a former bed of the river Gascorán forms the *uti possidetis iuris* boundary depends, as a question of fact, on the assertion that the Goascorán formerly was running in that bed, and that at some date it abruptly changed its course to its present position. On this basis El Salvador's argument of law is that where a boundary is formed in the course of a river and the stream suddenly leaves its old bed and forms a new one, this process of 'avulsion' does not bring about a change in the boundary, which continues to follow the old channel. No record of such an abrupt change of course having occurred has been brought to the Chamber's attention, but where the Chamber is satisfied that the river's course was earlier so radically different from its present one, then an avulsion might reasonably be inferred. While the area is low and swampy, so that different channels might well receive different proportions of the total run-off at different times, there does not seem to be a possibility of the change having occurred slowly by erosion and accretion, to which, as El Salvador concedes, different legal rules apply".

199 Apparently, in this sector three tributaries (the Mekrou, the Alibori and the Sota) enter the River Niger from the right bank, as a result of which it floods twice a year, in January–March and in September–October. Supra, note 83, p. 18, para. 104.

200 Ibid., p. 134, para. 108.

to the accretion of sediments and the trend of marine streams. In addition, Nicaragua argued that the instability and fluctuations of the river mouth were liable of continuing and causing changes in the co-ordinates of the terminus of the land boundary.[201] The Court acknowledged the existence of such accretion and the active morpho-dynamism that the delta of the River Coco exhibited as a result.[202] Based upon this natural phenomenon, it concluded that the accretion rendered it impossible to identify base points and construct a provisional equidistance line for the single maritime boundary delimiting maritime areas off the parties' mainland coasts.[203]

In the recent award in *Bay of Bengal Maritime Boundary Arbitration between Bangladesh and India*, Bangladesh argued that the River Hariabhanga and its main channel had changed significantly over the past seven decades and thus could not be considered as the terminus of the land boundary.[204] Opposing this contention, India postulated that successive maps and satellite imagery showed a remarkable stability in the profile of the Estuary and the location of its rivers.[205] Whilst accepting the possibility of a change in the river course, the tribunal disregarded such fact since it did not prevent it from locating the boundary terminus as it was in 1947, the critical date.[206]

Lately, in the cases of *Costa Rica* v. *Nicaragua* and *Nicaragua* v. *Costa Rica*, the Court was called upon to interpret the terms of the Treaty of Limits of 1848 and the Cleveland and Alexander Awards, which established the boundary between the two states. In this respect, both the Cleveland and Alexander Awards foresaw the possibility of not only gradual expansion or contraction of the banks of the San Juan River, but also overall changes in its channel. These awards prescribed that such changes would be regulated "on a case-by-case basis in accordance with such principles of international law as may be applicable".[207] Nicaragua argued that, as a result of natural modifications taking place over a number of years in the geographical configuration of the disputed territory, one of the channels under discussion connected the San Juan River with the southern tip of the Harbor Head Lagoon in such a

201 *Territorial and Maritime Dispute between Nicaragua and Honduras in the Caribbean Sea (Nicaragua* v. *Honduras), Judgment, I.C.J. Reports 2007*, p. 659, at p. 692, para. 99.

202 Ibid., p. 742, para. 277.

203 Ibid., pp. 743–744, para. 280.

204 Supra, note 158, p. 42, para. 147.

205 Ibid., p. 43, para. 151.

206 Ibid., p. 49, para. 173.

207 See, in particular, the second Alexander Award, *Reports of International Arbitral Awards*, Vol. XXVIII, p. 224.

way that it now marked the boundary and consequently placed the disputed territory under its sovereignty.[208] Contrary to this position, Costa Rica contended that there had been no significant shifting of the bed of the main channel of the Lower San Juan River since the Alexander Awards. Furthermore, it claimed that no importance should be given to what it considered to be an artificial channel (caño), which was excavated by Nicaragua in 2010 in order to connect the San Juan River with the Harbor Head Lagoon.[209] The Court arrived at the conclusion that there was not sufficient evidence to prove that a natural channel linked the San Juan River with the Harbor Head Lagoon that followed the same course as the channel that had been dredged by Nicaragua.[210]

2 The Phenomenon of the 'Walking Islands'

Natural alterations can also impact the fate of islands. As a matter of fact, islands in rivers are exposed to geological factors such as accretion and erosion in the waters of the river where they are located. In addition, the strong flow rate of a river may cause the deposit on the islands of suspended sediments, which are carried along the watercourse.[211] Furthermore, islands in rivers are vulnerable to climatological factors, such as strong floods or a period of heavy rains. All these circumstances may cause manifold issues concerning the river boundary and sovereignty over its islands.

Concerning geological factors, the flow rate of a river can cause the erosion of an island in its upstream area with the consequent deposit of its sediments

---

208 *Costa Rica* v. *Nicaragua* and *Nicaragua* v. *Costa Rica* cases, supra, note 99, p. 39, para. 78.

209 Ibid., p. 39, para. 77.

210 Ibid., p. 40, para. 81. The Court further stated "that the existence over a significant span of time of a navigable caño in the location claimed by Nicaragua is put into question by the fact that in the bed of the channel there were trees of considerable size and age which had been cleared by Nicaragua in 2010. Moreover, as was noted by Costa Rica's main expert, if the channel had been a distributary of the San Juan River, 'sediment would have filled in, or at a minimum partially-filled, the southern part of the lagoon'. Furthermore, the fact that, as the Parties' experts agree, the caño dredged in 2010 no longer connected the river with the lagoon by mid-summer 2011 casts doubt on the existence over a number of years of a navigable channel following the same course before Nicaragua carried out its dredging activities" (ibid., p. 41, para. 90).

211 Actually, sedimentation is quite frequent in both the Paraguay and Paraná Rivers, both part of the Plata Basin. The largest erosions take place in the upper basin of the Bermejo River, a tributary of the Paraguay River, in the Andean region of Argentina and Bolivia, Cordeiro, N. V., 'Environmental management issues in the Plata Basin', Biswas, A. K., et al. (eds.), *Management of Latin American River Basins: Amazon, Plata and São Francisco* (Tokyo: United Nations University Press, 1999), p. 151.

in its downstream zone. As a result of this geological change, the island will appear to the human eye as having lost its surface on one part of it, and as having simultaneously gained surface on another. If this phenomenon takes place for a number of years and an aero-photometrical assessment of the area in question is completed, the photograph will show that the island has actually moved, as though it has literally walked downstream. In such cases it becomes necesssary to determine what the legal effects of such a movement would be, particularly in those cases where the shift causes the island in question to be situated in the territory of the other co-riparian state.

There is not one single answer to this query.[212] It may well happen that there are certain islands which have been delimited according to a general rule applicable to all of the islands. In this case, effectiveness enters the scene. The factual situation existing prior to the natural alteration that resulted in the island 'walking' across the boundary line of the river should be applicable as a general rule. It is self-evident, however, that more often than not a controversy may arise between co-riparian states as to the sovereignty of the island in question. Therefore, it is advisable to resort to the competent boundary commission—or whatever organ with sufficient capacity to enforce the boundary treaty there may be—so that the islands of the river in question are adjudicated as appertaining to one or the other state.

When the possible 'walking islands' have already been identified and adjudicated as appertaining to one of the co-riparian states by the boundary treaty, the panorama is not only clearer, but further disputes can also be avoided if any of those islands actually 'walked'.[213] The Boundary Treaty of 3 February 1876 between Paraguay and Argentina is particularly illustrative in this respect.[214] This agreement regulates the situation of the islands, which are situated on both the Paraná and Paraguay Rivers. Articles 1 and 3 of the said treaty establish that, whilst the island of Yaciretá falls under Paraguayan sovereignty, those of Cerrito and Apipé belong to Argentina. Article 3 further stipulates that the rest of the islands will appertain to one co-riparian state or the other according

212 Cf. Philippe, C., 'La prise en compte des îles', *in*, Aurescu, B. & Pellet, A. (eds.), *Actualité du droit des fleuves internationaux* (Paris: Pedone, 2010), p. 51.

213 Such is the case of the Treaty of 7 April 1961 for the River Uruguay between Argentina and Uruguay, which identifies each of the islands of the river, and consequently adjudicates each one of them as appertaining to either one or the other state. See supra, note 67. The same solution appears in the Treaty of 21 January 1929 between Haiti and the Dominican Republic, which expressly stipulates that a number of islands appertain to the Dominican Republic, League of Nations, *League of Nations Treaty Series*, Vol. 105, pp. 193–213.

214 Parry, C., *Consolidated Treaty Series*, Vol. 150, p. 248 et seq.

to the particular island's adjacency to the territory of one of them. Therefore, the legal status of those islands that have already been adjudicated, i.e. Apipé, Cerrito and Yaciretá, remains unaltered, even if they have moved. As for the rest of the islands, the first solution described above should be applied in order to determine the legal status of those islands. An interesting fact in the matter under study is that a number of years after the entry into force of the Treaty of 1876 between Argentina and Paraguay, the island of Yaciretá split into two: one part continued to be known as Yaciretá and the other part was named Talavera. The issue then arose as to what was the legal status of the new island. If the general rule of contiguity was applied, Talavera Island should belong to Argentina. However, as the island of Talavera was a part of the former Yaciretá that had been expressly adjudicated as appertaining to Paraguay by a conventional rule, the co-riparian states regarded this new island as Paraguayan as well.

II *Human Activities Affecting an International River*

Besides natural alterations, human activities can also act on the geomorphological configuration of a boundary watercourse, thus affecting the boundary line. Co-riparian states may decide to intervene in their boundary river, consequently altering its course or one of the banks of the watercourse in question, just to mention some of the possible changes. With the aim of optimising the uses of their boundary watercourse, states can build up dams for hydroelectric power, divert waters for irrigation purposes or build new channels along the watercourse in question for all intents and purposes. From the moment a human being intervenes in nature, there is an impact indeed, which in our case can result in a variation of the river or lake boundary.

Once again, the consensual basis of the rules regulating international boundary watercourses is key to understanding the legal consequences of the subject under discussion. More often than not, when riparian states agree to perform work in their boundary watercourse, they foresee the possible modification in the boundary line as well. Hence, as long as both states have agreed on the realization of works in the river, even when these could result in alterations, no legal issue should arise, in principle.

As a result, a state is not entitled to make any alteration in the river which may result in a modification of its course, and consequently of the river boundary, in the absence of the previous consent of its co-riparian. In the first of the *Costa Rica* v. *Nicaragua* and *Nicaragua* v. *Costa Rica* cases, *Certain Activities Carried Out by Nicaragua in the Border Area*, Costa Rica claimed that Nicaragua had artificially excavated a channel in the San Juan River, in order to connect it to the Harbor Head Lagoon, and, as a result, affect the river boundary between the two states. On the contrary, Nicaragua claimed that it was only dredging an existing channel, which, due to natural circumstances had produced such connection between the river and the aforementioned lagoon. The International Court of Justice, however, dismissed this argument.[215]

Altering the river course in some way or another entails diversion, which, in as far as it is unilateral, results in a breach of the two substantive general customary norms regulating the use of international fresh watercourses: the no-harm rule and that of equitable utilization of the watercourse. Moreover, many boundary agreements expressly prevent the co-riparian states from altering in any way the international river that serves as a boundary between them, without the consent of the other state.[216] The procedural obligation to notify the other co-riparian state operates irrespective of the compliance of the substantive obligations described above. Acting in violation of such provisions is tantamount to a breach of an international legal obligation, resulting from the rules of international state responsibility and the application of its pertinent norms.[217]

III *Bridges and Other Works on Rivers*

The case of bridges and tunnels on rivers also raises questions as to the boundary line and its consequences in terms of sovereignty of the co-riparian states.[218] Since the basis of the legal regime in this regard is consensual, it is not suprising to find differing and opposing solutions on the subject.[219]

According to a general rule of international law, boundaries project themselves vertically both upwards into the aerial space and downwards into the underground.[220] When a bridge is built over an international river or a tunnel

---

215 See supra, note 99.

216 Cf. Bouchez, supra, note 21, p. 812. See the Treaty of 1848 between the United States and Mexico, supra, note 193.

217 The Institut de droit international, in its session of Madrid in 1911, laid down the norm that when a river amounts to an international boundary between two states, neither of them is entitled to do or let its nationals do any activity that may affect the river boundary.

218 See, in particular, Bauer, K., 'Grenzen an Straβenbrücken uber Grenzflüsse', *Zeitschrift für Wasserrecht*, Vol. 15(2) (1976), pp. 259–266.

219 Cf. Schröter, supra, note 15, pp. 978–979. See also Caflisch, supra, note 2, pp. 92–94 and Dipla, supra, note 95, pp. 619–620.

220 Article 5 of the Treaty of 29 February 1972 between Austria and Germany on their common boundaries expressly stipulates this rule: "Durch die Staatsgrenze werden die Hoheitsgebiete der beiden Vertragsstaaten sowhol auf der Erdoberfläche als auch in lotrechter Richtung im Luftraum und unter der Erdoberfläche voneinander abgegrenzt". *Bundesgesetzblatt*, Vol. II (1975), p. 767.

is made on its riverbed, one might then think that the boundary in the tunnel or bridge in question follows the boundary line chosen by the co-riparian states in the river. In line with this idea, the boundary line between the two states would separate two different territories that would project themselves both upwards and downwards from the river boundary.

However, state practice shows that this is not necessarily the case. It can either happen that these works have their own boundary independent from that of the river, or that they adjust to the boundary of the river. Both solutions have been envisaged in practice. Thus, there is in this respect a departure from the general rule, which would operate in that case as a modification of the general norm by a succeeding conventional one.[221]

When it has been agreed that the boundary in the bridge or tunnel corresponds to that of the international river that either lies beneath or surrounds the work in question, multiple scenarios are possible. Along this line, it may well happen that the mentioned work is adjudicated as belonging to a single state, particularly in those cases where the international river has been delimited by resorting to a single riverbank.[222] This is indeed the solution that has been implemented for the three bridges that cross the Morge, between Switzerland and France. As the boundary line is the riverbank, the bridges appertain accordingly to France. However, it can also occur that the bridge or tunnel is a *condominium* because that is precisely the boundary chosen for the international river. If the system of delimitation chosen by the riparian states is the *thalweg*, one might well wonder what happens in the event of a shift in this boundary. In the *Benin/Niger* case, the International Court of Justice ruled that the boundary between Benin and Niger on the bridges between Gaya and Malanville follows the course of the boundary in the River Niger, which is the *thalweg*.[223] In this respect, it has been argued that it would not be logical to choose a correspondence between both boundaries—i.e. that of the bridge or tunnel and that of the international river—to change it later.[224] Still, riparian states are always free to agree on a different solution.[225] In conclusion, in all the examples described above there is a coincidence between both boundaries.

The second possibility available for co-riparian states is that of autonomous boundaries for the international river on the one hand, and for the works that have been made over it, on the other. In this case, the boundary will lie at the

221 Cf. Barberis, supra, note 3, p. 158.

222 See the Treaty of 10 June 1891 *in*, Parry, C., *Consolidated Treaty Series*, Vol. 175, p. 169 et seq.

223 Supra, note 83, p. 151, para. 146.

224 Schröter, supra, note 15, p. 979.

225 Dipla, supra, note 95, p. 619.

middle of the bridge or of the tunnel, independently from the boundary of the river in question.[226] This seems in our mind only logical. From the moment we consider that both co-riparian states may use the bridge for obvious considerations of communication with all the consequences that this entails, this appears as the more equitable solution. In this way, both states will bear the costs of maintenance and administration of the work on an equal basis and not only proportionally, as would be the case for the river boundary. Furthermore, in all the cases where autonomous and independent boundaries are preferred, it is important to bear in mind that the boundary between both co-riparian states from a territorial point of view will always be one: its only peculiarity will be that of its form. Indeed, it will amount to an oblique boundary line when it goes up from—or down from—the river to the work in question. Ultimately, there is only one boundary line from a territorial standpoint, not two. It is merely its projection upwards or downwards in a plane that varies in the latter case examined.

Part 3: Particularities in International Rivers and Lakes

I *Enclaves in International Rivers and Lakes*

Enclaves are undoubtedly a singularity in international river and lake delimitation. They amount to a particular case of a state territory which is discontinuous. They consist of a part of a territory of one state, which is detached from the rest of the territory of that state and is entirely surrounded by the territory of another state.[227] If the whole territory of a state is surrounded by the entire territory of another, then it is not an enclave. The surrounded territory in question must be part of the territory of another state in order to qualify as the figure under study.

Enclaves can be surrounded both by land and/or water. In the latter case, they amount to insular enclaves, which are present in international lakes, rivers or the territorial sea of a certain state.

---

226 See the Treaty of 30 January 1963 between France and Germany on the Rhine *in*, Bauer, supra, note 218, p. 262 et seq.

227 Cf. Charpentier, J., 'Le problème des enclaves', *in*, Société française de droit intenational (ed.), *La frontière*, Colloque de Poitiers (Paris: Pedone, 1980), p. 41. On enclaves in general, see Raton, P., 'Les enclaves', *Annuaire française de droit international* (1958), p. 186 et seq. More recently, Irmscher, T. M., 'Enclaves', *in*, *Encylopedia of Public International Law*, www.opil.ouplaw.com/home/EPIL. Accessed on 15 January 2016.

Fluvial and lacustrine enclaves are generally regulated on a conventional basis, thus, previously agreed by the co-riparian states. Therefore, they can only be examined on a case-by-case approach. The 1961 Boundary Treaty between Argentina and Uruguay provides an example of this.[228] Article 1, paragraph B, II of this treaty prescribes two diverse boundary lines in the area of the river where the Filomena and Medio channels bifurcate. Whereas the former amounts to the boundary as to the waters, the latter constitutes the boundary line with respect to islands. Consequently, some islands such as Filomena Chica, Filomena Grande, Palma Chica, Bassi and Tres Cruces are tantamount to Uruguayan enclaves surrounded by Argentine waters.

Likewise, the Boundary Treaty of 3 February 1876 between Argentina and Paraguay establishes two different boundary lines for the waters and for the islands of the Paraná River. Whilst, according to Article 1 of the agreement, the boundary for the waters is the *thalweg*, Article 3 stipulates that attribution of the islands will be based on the median line.[229] But since the *thalweg* of the river runs very close to the Argentine coast, there are some islands which are close to that coast but still separated from it by the *thalweg*. As a result, there are several Argentine islands which are completely surrounded by Paraguayan waters. Such is the case with the island Entre Ríos, the six islands of the Caa Verá group, the Islas Verdes and the two islands of Costa Larga.

In addition, the Treaty of 18 June 1954 establishes the legal regime of the Chisamulo and Likoma Islands in Lake Malawi.[230] These islands fall under the sovereignty of Malawi. However, they lie near the eastern bank of the lake, surrounded by waters under the sovereignty of Mozambique. The main reason in this case is historical: at the time when Malawi was a British colony—Nyassaland—British missionaries first occupied the island of Likoma and built there the first cathedral of the colony. Later on, this situation was further consolidated. Thus, when the mentioned agreement of 1954 was negotiated between Great Britain and Portugal, the latter could not oppose the existence of a close tie between this island and Nyassaland. As a result, both Likoma and Chisamulo were established as British enclaves inside Portuguese territory. Similar to what happens concerning maritime islands, it was agreed that a belt of two sea miles would surround each of these islands.[231] The rest

228 United Nations, *United Nations Treaty Series*, Vol. 635, p. 92 et seq.

229 Parry, C., *Consolidated Treaty Series*, Vol. 150, p. 248 et seq.

230 See supra, note 109.

231 Paragraph 2 of Article 1 of the mentioned treaty stipulates: "The Government of the United Kingdom shall retain sovereignty over the islands of Chisamulo and Likoma, together with the exercise of all rights flowing from such sovereignty, including full, unrestricted

of the waters of the lake were delimited according to the median line. Hence, despite the portion of 'British water' granted to the islands in question, they are still bordered by Portuguese waters.[232]

On the contrary, there is no conventional instrument that foresees the rules to be applied to Campione de Italia, a half lake, half terrestrial enclave. Situated in the Swiss lake, Lake Locarno, Campione was a donation from Charlemagne to the Saint Ambrose Foundation of Milan. Switzerland accepted this fact from the beginning, letting Italian officials and civilians traverse Swiss waters to get to the enclave under analysis. From this practice, we can deduce a bilateral customary rule, as far as the right of passage to the enclave is concerned.

The legal norms applicable to enclaves are *grosso modo* the same as those which regulate sovereignty over land. Above all, the state whose territory is tantamount to an enclave should be assured the possibility to exercise all its sovereign rights. Consequently, neighbourly relations among riparian states are emphasised, together with the inherent right of passage across the part of the lake that corresponds to the other state whose waters surround the enclave in question. Notwithstanding their peculiar character, the importance of enclaves in watercourses should not be overlooked. Whilst state territory is generally composed of a unified and continuous space, uninterrupted by the territory of other states, enclaves may appear, and not only due to historical reasons underlying the constitution of a certain state. Enclaves could also provide an answer to complex boundary conflicts among co-riparian states, especially those with a strong ethnic composition. Hence, alongside existing enclaves resulting from historical circumstances, there could be new enclaves constituting a compromise solution to long-term disputes over boundaries in rivers and lakes among neighbouring states.

Part 4: The Role of Human Considerations in International River and Lake Delimitation

I *Human Freshwater Needs and Access to Water*

While disregarded in the past, human considerations—i.e. human freshwater needs—seem to have lately acquired a more active role in international

---

and unconditional rights of access. The Government of the United Kingdom shall also retain sovereignty over a belt of water two sea miles in width surrounding each of these islands (…)", United Nations, *United Nations Treaty Series*, Vol. 325, p. 310. For an analysis of this enclave, see Pondaven, supra, note 11, pp. 110–111 and 114–115.

232 See, in this respect, Charpentier, supra, note 227, p. 47 et seq.

river and lake delimitation. The latest judicial and arbitral jurisprudence on the subject confirms this view. As a matter of fact, the most recent cases in this respect reveal how water-related interests of riparian communities are being taken increasingly into account in the establishment of boundary lines in rivers and lakes. In this regard, human considerations continue to steadily permeate the international legal order as a whole.[233] The pertinent norms in the field of international river and lake delimitation are not immune to such 'humanization'.

Co-riparian states negotiate and agree in their respective delimitation treaties on a certain type of boundary line instead of others in the light of the different uses envisaged for the international watercourse in question, considering in particular the practices of its national riparian inhabitants. In doing so, it remains crucial to ensure access to water of their respective local communities for various purposes, thus guaranteeing the subsistence of those communities. This latter aspect has more often than not provided an argument for several states in support of their territorial claims in frontier and delimitation disputes before international tribunals. In addition, international tribunals no longer dismiss so promptly, and have even started actively incorporating, human considerations as a basis in their decisions on land boundary delimitations, and especially with regard to those based on fresh watercourses. In this respect, it is worth analyzing and distinguishing those cases where human needs were used as an argument to support the claim for a certain boundary line in an international watercourse, and those other cases where an international tribunal actually mentioned them as relevant considerations in a judgment.

Along this line, in the *Kasikili/Sedudu Island* case, Namibia based its claim of its sovereignty over the Kasikili/Sedudu Island in the Chobe River on the grazing and agricultural rights of the Masubia tribe over the island. The Court analyzed whether this intermittent presence of the Masubians and their practice of cultivating land on the island could amount to a subsequent practice in the interpretation of the applicable 1890 boundary treaty between Namibia

233 Meron refers to the radiation or reforming effect of human rights in other fields of international law. Cf., Meron, Th., 'International Law in the Age of Human Rights. General Course of Public International Law', *Recueil des cours de l'Académie de droit international de la Haye*, Vol. 301 (2003), p. 22. See also Cassesse, A., *The Human Dimension of International Law: Selected Papers* (Oxford: Oxford University Press, 2008), 642 p. and Weiss, N. & Thouvenin, J-M. (eds.), *The Influence of Human Rights in International Law* (Cham: Springer, 2015), p. 248.

and Botswana.[234] However, it dismissed this claim on the basis that no link could be inferred from such practice and the claim of the Caprivi authorities (Namibia) over the island and consequently ruled that the island formed part of the territory of Botswana.[235]

In the *Bay of Bengal Maritime Boundary Arbitration between Bangladesh and India*, the states concerned disagreed on the location of the land boundary terminus, which was to be determined by application of the Radcliffe Award of 1947 that drew the boundaries between India and Pakistan. In this respect, Bangladesh argued that the equitable considerations, as well as social or economic factors, adduced by India during the oral stage of the proceedings were irrelevant in determining the location of the boundary terminus for interpreting the wording of the Radcliffe Award. The tribunal concluded that the uses of the rivers shed no light on the question and that neither party had adduced sufficient evidence in this regard.[236]

In the recent *Costa Rica* v. *Nicaragua* and *Nicaragua* v. *Costa Rica* cases, Nicaragua alleged that the construction of a road near the riverbank of the San Juan River by Costa Rica had had an adverse impact on the health of the riparian communities, which was dependent upon the health of the river itself.[237] Unlike the cases examined so far, where the dispute directly concerned the boundary line of a certain watercourse, here the issue at stake was the environmental impact of certain activities alongside that type of boundary. This case is still relevant—at least incidentally—to the topic under study insofar as the International Court of Justice had once again the opportunity to examine the interests of local communities and their dependency on access to water—in this case to the San Juan River—as part of the argument in favour of Nicaragua's claim against Costa Rica. However, the Court found that Nicaragua had failed to substantiate its contention in this regard and therefore finally dismissed this argument.[238]

More recently, in its Application instituting proceedings against Bolivia with regard to a *Dispute over the Status and Use of the Waters of the Silala*, Chile claims that the River Silala is an international watercourse. Among other arguments, it supports its contention on the ground that

234 Supra, note 54, pp. 1093–1094, paras. 71–75.

235 Ibid., pp. 1106–1108, paras. 100–104.

236 Supra, note 158, p. 48, para. 167.

237 Supra, note 99, p. 72, para. 214.

238 Ibid., p. 73, para. 217.

> [t]he waters of the Silala River have historically and for more than a century been used in Chile for different purposes, including the provision of water supply to the city of Antofagasta and the towns of Sierra Gorda and Baquedano.[239]

In the above-examined cases, human freshwater needs were invoked as an argument of the states concerned to support their contentions with relation to a certain international watercourse and its boundary line. However, one might well wonder whether these human freshwater needs or human considerations have ever actually been mentioned as relevant considerations in a judgment. The *Dispute Regarding Navigational and Related Rights* case between Costa Rica and Nicaragua is emblematic in the matter under study. Not only did the International Court of Justice expressly recognize the right of fishing for subsistence purposes of the inhabitants of the Costa Rican bank of the San Juan River, but it also went even further and declared it constituted a local customary right.[240] With regard to the right of navigation foreseen in Article VI of the 1858 Treaty of Limits between the two states, the Court added that while its wording only expressly mentioned navigation for commercial purposes:

> [I]t cannot have been the intention of the authors of the 1858 Treaty to deprive the inhabitants of the Costa Rican bank of the river, where that bank constitutes the boundary between the two States, of the right to use the river to the extent necessary to meet their essential requirements, even for activities of a non-commercial nature, given the geography of the area.[241]

The Court further recognized the right of the inhabitants of the Costa Rican bank of the San Juan River to navigate on the river between the riparian communities for the purposes of the essential needs of everyday life requiring expeditious transportation.[242] This was later reaffirmed in the *Costa Rica* v. *Nicaragua* and *Nicaragua* v. *Costa Rica* cases.[243]

The recognition of access to the waters of an international river or lake by the local communities of riparian states was again expressly reaffirmed in the *Frontier Dispute* (*Burkina Faso/Niger*):

---

239 Supra, note 8, p. 3, para. 11.

240 Supra, note 101, pp. 265–266, para. 141.

241 Ibid., p. 246, para. 79.

242 Ibid., p. 270, para. 156(1)(f).

243 Supra, note 99, p. 53, para. 133.

> Moreover, the Court considers that there is no evidence before it that the River Sirba in the area of Bossébangou was attributed entirely to one of the two colonies. It notes in this regard that the requirement concerning access to water resources of all the people living in the riparian villages is better met by a frontier situated in the river than on one bank or the other.[244]

The Court further expressed its wish that both states take into consideration the needs of the populations concerned, in particular those of the nomadic and semi-nomadic populations and the necessity to overcome the difficulties that may arise for them because of the frontier.[245] In this case, human freshwater needs had a direct influence on the delimitation of the boundary in the River Sirba by the International Court of Justice. On the contrary, in the *Dispute Regarding Navigational and Related Rights* case, the Court recognized access rights to Costa Rica to the waters of the San Juan River, to make up for a boundary line that impeded access to this state.

From the moment the rule on reasonable and equitable utilization of international watercourses is a consecrated norm of general international law, co-riparian states are at least legally bound to take this norm into consideration during the delimitation process and not only after the boundary line in the watercourse has already been established.[246] The recognition of human considerations indeed favours the negotiation and conclusion of agreements on international river and lake delimitation in the light of reasonable and equitable use. The techniques chosen to delimit boundaries in international rivers and lakes seek to realize equity while providing for individual solutions

244 Supra, note 119, p. 85, para. 101. In his Separate Opinion, Judge Cançado Trindade expressed further in this respect: "The basic lesson I extract from the present case of the Frontier Dispute between Burkina Faso and Niger is that—as the present Judgment of the ICJ shows—it is perfectly warranted and viable to determine a frontier line keeping in mind the needs of the local populations. In the cas d'espèce, the contending Parties themselves, disclosing a commendable spirit of procedural co-operation, have provided the Court with the elements needed for its determination, taking into account people and territory together. Both Burkina Faso and Niger have expressed their common concern with the local populations (on both sides of their border and constantly moving across it) in their arguments before the Court in the written and oral phases of the proceedings. They have expressed their common concern with the villages in the region, focusing on territory and their inhabitants together". (Ibid., Separate Opinion of Judge Cançado Trindade, p. 131, para. 99).

245 Ibid., para. 112.

246 Forteau, supra, note 55, p. 33.

adapted to the particular circumstances of each watercourse.[247] Through such means, human considerations play a central role, which the most recent jurisprudence has acknowledged.[248] Whilst arguments favouring a certain delimitation method on the basis of such human considerations have sometimes been dismissed for lack of sufficient evidence, it cannot be denied that those considerations are nowadays recognized as such. International tribunals readily take due regard of the practices of riparian inhabitants of international rivers and lakes and the need to ensure their access to water for subsistence purposes. Furthermore, such access has even been recognized as a local customary norm in the case of the San Juan River.

Through the recognition of human considerations, contemporary international law tends to ensure the increasingly equitable and reasonable character of fluvial and lacustrine delimitation.[249] By seeking to assure access of their respective local communities to the waters of a boundary river or lake, co-riparian states are not only favouring the reasonable and equitable use of that fresh watercourse. They are also complying with their obligations to respect and guarantee the realization of the human right to water, which will be analyzed in the following section.

Human considerations have proven to amount to key elements both in treaty interpretation for lake and river delimitation and in the recognition of new customary norms in this area.

II *The Human Right to Water and Its Influence in the Field of Delimitation*

On 28 July 2010, the United Nations General Assembly adopted a resolution in which it recognized "the right to safe and clean drinking water and sanitation

---

247 Muller, A., 'The Delimitation of Boundary River Waters', *Thesaurus Acroasium*, Vol. XIV (1985), pp. 671–672.

248 Kohen and Tignino have identified *Land, Island and Maritime Frontier Dispute (El Salvador/ Honduras: Nicaragua intervening)* as the first case in which states have developed arguments regarding the human factor as a basis for territorial delimitation. In the said case, the Chamber of the Court discarded these arguments. Still, the human factor and impact of this aspect on boundary delimitation have been addressed in cases in which a judge or arbitrator is entitled to decide *ex aequo et bono* (Kohen, M. & Tignino, M., 'Do people have rights in boundaries' delimitations?', *in*, Boisson de Chazournes, L. et al. (eds.), *International Law and Freshwater: The Multiple Challenges* (Cheltenham: Edward Elgar Publishing Ltd., 2013), p. 101.

249 Along this line, Forteau declares: "Il est impossible de vouloir séparer aujourd'hui ce qui relève de la délimitation de ce qui relève de l'utilisation du fleuve", Forteau, supra, note 55, p. 39.

as a human right that is essential for the full enjoyment of life and all human rights".[250]

General Comment No. 15 of the Committee on Economic, Social and Cultural Rights (CESCR) on the right to water defines this right as entitling everyone "to sufficient, safe, accessible, physically accessible and affordable water for personal and domestic uses".[251] It also stresses that water is a "limited natural resource and a public good fundamental to life and health".[252] This document has indeed played a crucial role in the emergence of the human right to water and its further development.[253] States must respect, protect and fulfil this right.[254] The obligation to respect requires states to refrain from interfering directly or indirectly with the enjoyment of the right to water.

1 The Legal Nature of the Human Right to Water

a) *Treaty Norms*

The Committee on Economic, Social and Cultural Rights (CESCR) analyzes the human right to water within the scope of Article 11, paragraph 1 of the International Covenant on Economic, Social and Cultural Rights (ICESCR), which foresees the right of everyone to an adequate standard of living.[255] This article contemplates a series of rights deriving or being inferred from the right to an adequate standard of living, which are necessary for the latter's realization. Although the norm does not explicitly mention water alongside the rights to food, housing and adequate clothing, the term 'including' in its wording reveals the non-exhaustive character of the list it provides. Rather it is meant to include other implicit and derived rights that are necessary as well to

250 United Nations, A/64/L.63.

251 United Nations, E/C.12/2002/11, p. 2, para. 2.

252 Cf. Article 27 of the International Covenant on Economic, Social and Cultural Rights (ICESCR), United Nations, *United Nations Treaty Series*, Vol. 993, p. 3 et seq. The ICESCR was adopted on 16 November 1966 and has been in force since 3 January 1976.

253 Cf. Winkler, I. T., *The Human Right to Water: Significance, Legal Status and Implications for Water Allocation* (Oxford: Hart Publishing Ltd., 2012), p. 38.

254 Cf. paragraphs 21 to 36 of General Comment No. 15 of the ICESCR Committee.

255 This article states: "The States Parties to the present Covenant recognize the right of everyone to an adequate standard of living for himself and his family, including adequate food, clothing and housing, and to the continuous improvement of living conditions. The States Parties will take appropriate steps to ensure the realization of this right, recognizing to this effect the essential importance of international co-operation based on free consent".

pursue an adequate standard of living.[256] Hence, inasmuch as it is fundamental for the survival of every human being, the right to food derives and helps ensure the said standard. In this respect, Article 11 of the ICESCR takes up the wording of Article 25, paragraph 1 of the Universal Declaration of Human Rights.[257] Therefore, as part of the right to an adequate standard of living, the right to water is a legal norm, binding upon states parties to the ICESCR. The diverse existing cultural and social conditions of each particular case should be taken into account when evaluating what is to be considered an adequate standard.

The right to water is also inextricably linked to paragraph 1 of Article 12 of the ICESCR prescribing the right of everyone to the enjoyment of the highest attainable standard of physical and mental health. Whereas the Covenant cannot, evidently, assure the right to be healthy, this right is to be understood as "a right to the enjoyment of a variety of facilities, goods, services and conditions necessary for the realization of the highest attainable standard of health".[258] As such, it comprises several "socio-economic factors that promote conditions in which people can lead a healthy life, and extends to the underlying determinants of health". Access to safe and potable water is indeed an underlying determinant of the right to health.[259]

Besides the ICESCR, other treaties recognize the right to water and sanitation. This is the case with Article 14 of the Convention on the Elimination of All Forms of Discrimination Against Women,[260] Article 24 of the Convention

---

256 Salman, S. M. A. & McInerney-Lankford, S., *The Human Right to Water: Legal and Policy Dimensions* (Washington: The World Bank, 2004), p. 56. Cf. Gleick, P., 'The Human Right to Water', *Water Policy*, Vol. 1 (1998), p. 492. Also, Querol, M., 'The Human Right to Water and Sanitation: The Challenges of Its Application in Latin America', *in*, Rey Caro, E. & Rodriguez de Taborda, M. C. (eds.), *Estudios de Derecho Internacional en Homenaje a la Dra. Zlata Drnas de Clément* (Córdoba: Advocatus, 2014), pp. 757–786.

257 This article affirms: "Everyone has the right to a standard of living adequate for the health and well-being of himself and of his family, including food, clothing, housing and medical care and necessary social services, and the right to security in the event of unemployment, sickness, disability, widowhood, old age or other lack of livelihood in circumstances beyond his control."

258 Cf. General Comment No. 14, The Right to the Highest Attainable Standard of Health (Article 12 of the Internationational Covenant on Economic, Social and Cultural Rights), United Nations, E/C.12/2000/4, para. 9.

259 McCaffrey, S., 'The Human Right to Water', *in*, Brown Weiss, E.; Boisson de Chazournes, L., & Bernasconi-Osterwalder, N. (eds.), *Fresh Water and International Economic Law* (New York: Oxford University Press, 2005), p. 95.

260 Article 14 states that states shall take all appropriate measures to eliminate discrimination against women in rural areas. They shall ensure to such women the right to "enjoy adequate living conditions, particularly in relation to housing, sanitation, electricity and

on the Rights of the Child,[261] Article 28 of the Convention on the Rights of Persons with Disabilities[262] and Article 5 of the 1985 C161 ILO Occupational Health Services Convention.[263]

At a regional level, both Article 14 of the African Charter on the Rights and Welfare of the Child and Article 15 of the Protocol to the African Charter on Human and Peoples Rights (also known as the Banjul Charter) on the Rights of Women in Africa, also known as the Maputo Protocol, prescribe access to safe-drinking water.[264]

International humanitarian law also recognizes the right to water. Articles 20, 26, 29 and 46 of the Convention (III) relative to the Treatment of Prisoners at War prescribe the provision of safe-drinking water and facilities "which conform to the rules of hygiene and are maintained in a constant state of cleanliness" for those who have this status during an armed conflict.[265] In addition, Articles 85, 89 and 127 of Convention (IV) relative to the Protection of Civilians during Times of War contain similar provisions.[266] Norms relative to the right to water can also be found in both Additional Protocols I and II to the Geneva Conventions.[267]

---

water supply, transport and communications". United Nations, *United Nations Treaty Series*, Vol. 1246, p. 14 et seq.

261 Article 24 of this Convention recognizes the right of children to the enjoyment of the highest attainable standard of health (para. 1). "States Parties shall pursue full implementation of this right and, in particular, shall take appropriate measures: (…) To combat disease and malnutrition, including within the framework of primary health care, through, inter alia, (…) the provision of adequate nutritious foods and clean drinking-water" (para. 2(c)), United Nations, *United Nations Treaty Series*, Vol. 1577, p. 3 et seq.

262 Article 28 of this treaty recognizes the rights of persons with disabilities to an adequate standard of living for themselves and their families. In its paragraph 2(a) it imposes upon states the obligation to take measures to "ensure equal access by persons with disabilities to clean water services, and to ensure access to appropriate and affordable services, devices and other assistance for disability-related needs". United Nations, A/61/611.

263 C161 was adopted in Geneva on 25 June 1985 and has been in force since 17 February 1988. http://www.ilo.org/ilolex/cgi-lex/convds.pl?C161.

264 The African Charter on the Rights and Welfare of the Child entered into force on 29 November 1999. OAU, Doc. CAB/LEG/24.9/49 (1990). The Maputo Protocol was adopted by the Second Ordinary Session of the Assembly of the African Union on 13 September 2000 and entered into force on 25 November 2005. OAU, CAB/LEG/66.6. *Reprinted in, African Human Rights Law Journal*, Vol. 1, p. 40 et seq.

265 United Nations, *United Nations Treaty Series*, Vol. 75, p. 135 et seq.

266 United Nations, *United Nations Treaty Series*, Vol. 75, p. 287 et seq.

267 Cf. Articles 54 and 55 of Protocol I relating to the Protection of Victims of International Armed Conflicts. United Nations, *United Nations Treaty Series*, Vol. 1125, p. 3 et seq. See

International water law is not exempted from the subject under study. As analyzed above, Article 10, paragraph 1 of the 1997 UN Convention on the Law of the Non-Navigational Uses of International Watercourses states that, in the event of a conflict between different uses of an international watercourse, it shall be solved with "special regard being given to the requirements of vital human needs".[268] The 1999 Protocol on Water and Health to the 1992 Convention on the Protection and Use of Transboundary Watercourses and International Lakes of the United Nations Economic Commission for Europe (also known as the Water Convention) has particularly promoted the recognition of the right to water.[269] In Africa, the 2002 Water Charter of the Senegal River specifically foresees "basic human rights to a salubrious water"[270] as part of the rights and guiding principles to be respected in any distribution of the waters of the river. This right is also expressly proclaimed at a Latin American level in the 2006 Central American Water Covenant.[271]

b) *Standards and Non-binding Rules*

Numerous 'soft' or non-binding instruments have similarly triggered the consecration of the human right to water and sanitation. The Action Plan from the United Nations Water Conference was the first to recognize—already in 1977—the right to water by declaring that "[A]ll peoples, whatever their stage of development and social and economic conditions, have the right to have access to drinking water in quantities and of a quality equal to their basic needs".[272] Chapter 18 of the Rio 21 Agenda followed the lead undertaken by

---

also Article 5, paragraph 1(b) and Article 14 of Protocol II relating to the Protection of Victims of Non-International Armed Conflicts. United Nations, *United Nations Treaty Series*, Vol. 1125, p. 609 et seq.

268 This Convention was adopted by United Nations Resolution A/RES/51/229 of 21 May 1997. Since it is not yet in force, its norms are not legally binding as treaty norms. Nevertheless, many of its provisions also possess a customary nature.

269 The Protocol on Water and Health was adopted on 17 June 1999 and entered into force on 4 August 2005. United Nations, *United Nations Treaty Series*, Vol. 2331, p. 202. See, in particular, Article 6, paragraph 1(a).

270 Article 4 of this treaty, which was adopted by Mauritania, Mali and Senegal on 28 May 2002. http://lafrique.free.fr/traites/omvs_200205.pdf (official text in French). Accessed on 21 May 2016.

271 This treaty was adopted within the framework of the Central American Integration System by all states of the region on 11 August 2006.

272 Resolution II (Community Water Supply), para. (a), United Nations, UN Doc. No. E/CONF. 70/29, *Report of the United Nations Water Conference*, Mar del Plata, 14–25 March 1977, United Nations Publication, Sales No. E.77.II. A.12.

its predecessor. It is based on the premise of the International Drinking Water Supply and Sanitation Decade, which establishes that "all peoples, whatever their stage of development and their social and economic conditions, have the right to have access to drinking water in quantities and of a quality equal to their basic needs".[273] Furthermore, it sets the general goal of ensuring universal access to safe drinking water and universal access to sanitary measures of excreta disposal, thereby markedly reducing waterborne diseases such as cholera and schistosomiasis.[274]

Along the same line, the 1992 Dublin Declaration on Water and Sustainable Development recognizes in its Principle 4 that "it is vital to recognize first the basic right of all human beings to have access to clean water and sanitation at an affordable price". In addition, the Programme of Action of the UN International Conference on Population and Development asserts in its Principle 2 that all individuals "[H]ave the right to an adequate standard of living for themselves and their families, including (…) water and sanitation".[275]

Moreover, building on the UN Millennium Declaration and its eight Millennium Development Goals (MDGs) (2000–2015), the 2030 Agenda for Sustainable Development includes a dedicated goal on water and sanitation (SDG 6) that sets out to "ensure availability and sustainable management of water and sanitation for all". SDG 6 expands the MDG focus on drinking water and basic sanitation to cover now the entire water cycle, including the management of water, wastewater and ecosystem resources. With water at the very core of sustainable development, SDG 6 not only has strong linkages to all of the other SDGs, but also the ability to underpin them. Also, the Johannesburg Declaration of the 2002 World Summit on Sustainable Development engages states to speedily increase access to basic requirements such as clean water and sanitation, among others.[276]

All these instruments have indeed contributed *de lege ferenda* to the recognition of the human right to water and sanitation. They amount to standards or *soft law* rules and thus, are not legally binding for the subjects of the international community. Nonetheless, they do produce certain legal effects, which should not be under-estimated. Above all, soft law contributes

273 United Nations, UN Doc. No. A/CONF.151/26/REV.1 (Vol. II), para. 18.47.

274 Ibid., para. 6.12(e).

275 United Nations, UN Doc. No. A/CONF.171/13 rev.1.

276 United Nations, A/CONF.199/20, Annex, para. 18.

to the interpretation of hard law.[277] It is important to consider, for example, the General Comments submitted periodically by the *Special Rapporteurs* of the former Sub-Commission—now the Human Rights Council Advisory Committee—and specialised committees on Human Rights. These documents assist states parties to human rights conventions in clarifying the scope and content of norms.[278] Such standards can also provide an authoritative interpretation of the terms of a treaty.[279]

'Soft law' can also foster and accelerate the formation of international legal norms.[280] The existence of most customary norms of human rights law has

277 Cf. Djena Wembou, M.-C., 'Réflexions sur le rôle des résolutions dans l'élaboration du droit international par les organes politiques de l'ONU', *Revue hellénique de droit international*, Vol. 45 (1992), p. 105.

278 Cf. Simma, B., 'International Human Rights and General International Law: A Comparative Analysis', *Collected Courses of the Academy of European Law*, Vol. 4, Book 2 (1993), p. 156.

279 Boyle, A. & Chinkin, Ch., *The Making of International Law* (Oxford: Oxford University Press, 2007), pp. 216–217. Judge Jiménez de Aréchaga confirmed this in his Separate Opinion in the *Continental Shelf* case between Tunisia and Libya. He wrote: "(…) Tunisia has advanced a somewhat broader interpretation of the clause in the Special Agreement. It observed that if such an interpretation is rigidly maintained, then 'the mention of this category in the Compromis would have added nothing to the principles and rules of international law' and consequently, this reference to 'new accepted trends' would have no legal effect at all. The submission was then made by Tunisia that even if a new accepted trend does not yet qualify as a rule of customary law, it still may have a bearing on the decision of the Court, not as part of applicable law, but as an element in the interpretation of existing rules or as an indication of the direction in which such rules should be interpreted. This is, in my opinion, the correct view of the Special Agreement and the only one which assigns practical effect and an independent meaning and significance to the reference to new accepted trends. As the Court has said, 'no method of interpretation would warrant the conclusion' that this reference is meaningless (*I.C.J. Reports 1971*, p. 35)". *Continental Shelf (Tunisia/Libyan Arab Jamahiriya), Judgment of 24 February 1982, Separate Opinion of Judge Jiménez de Aréchaga, I.C.J. Reports 1982*, p. 18, at p. 108, paras. 33–34. Judge Jiménez de Aréchaga's Separate Opinion in the *Continental Shelf* case confirms this view. Indeed, in this case Tunisia argued that the allusion of the Special Agreement to 'new trends' accepted at the Third UN Conference on the Law of the Sea, "do[es] not constitute general international law, [but] are to be taken into account as 'factors in the interpretation of the existing rules'", ibid., p. 38, para. 24.

280 Lachs, M., 'The Threshold in Law-Making', *in*, Bernhardt, R. et al. (eds.), *Völkerrecht als Rechtsordnung, Internationale Gerichtbarkeit, Menschenrechte, Festschrift für Hermann Mosler* (Berlin: Springer, 1983), p. 500. Cf. Francioni, F., 'International "Soft Law": A Contemporary Assessment', *in*, Lowe, V. (ed.), *Fifty Years of the International Court of*

been triggered by 'soft-law' standards.[281] States usually prefer to be looked upon as respectful of human rights, and standards exercise a constraining influence on them in this regard. They encompass the promotion of certain values and ideological considerations by which subjects of the international community prefer to abide. This is equally true in other areas of the international legal order such as environmental law. For example, the Helsinki Rules of 1966 have provided a great aid in the emergence of customary norms for the non-navigational uses of international watercourses.

Moreover, 'soft law' rules and standards play a role in the application of international legal norms. Standards operate as directives for an adequate fulfilment of international obligations.[282] They specify the manner in which states should comply with the obligations contained in a treaty, for example. Similarly, many international organizations provide standards for the implementation of their provisions. Hence, such standards can perform a supplemental function in developing conventional norms.[283]

c) *International Case Law*

The right to water and sanitation has also been addressed in the jurisprudence of international courts. In the *Pulp Mills on the River Uruguay* case, the International Court of Justice stresses the need to warrant the environmental protection of shared natural resources, simultaneously enabling sustainable economic development. In particular, it states that due consideration must be given to the dependence of the parties on the quality of river waters for their subsistence and economic development.[284]

Justice. Essays in Honour of Sir Robert Jennings (Cambridge: Cambridge University Press, 1996), p. 176.

281 Cf. Reisman, M., 'The Concept and Functions of Soft Law in International Politics', *in*, Bello, E. G. & Ajibola, P. B. A. (eds.), *Essays in Honour of Judge Taslim Olawale Elias. Contemporary International Law and Human Rights*, Vol. 1 (Dordrecht: Martinus Nijhoff, 1992), pp. 139–140.

282 Boyle, A. E., 'Some Reflections on the Relationship of Treaties and Soft Law', *International & Comparative Law Quarterly*, Vol. 48 (1999), p. 905.

283 Skubiszewski, K., 'Non-binding Resolutions and the Law-making Process', *Polish Yearbook of International Law*, Vol. 15 (1986), p. 151. In line with this idea, Boisson de Chazournes refers to the compensating or correcting function of standards. Boisson de Chazournes, L., 'Normes, standards et règles en droit international', *in*, *Les enjeux de la normalisation technique internationale. Entre environnement, santé et commerce international* (Paris: La documentation française, 2006), p. 47.

284 *Pulp Mills on the River Uruguay (Argentina* v. *Uruguay), Order of 13 July 2006, I.C.J. Reports 2006*, p. 133, para. 80.

The Inter-American Court of Human Rights has analyzed the human right to water on numerous occasions. In the *Case of the Sawhoyamaxa Indigenous Community v. Paraguay*, the Court decided that the Republic of Paraguay had failed to relocate the Sawhoyamaxa community to their ancestral lands where they would have the use and full enjoyment of the natural resources providing them the means to maintain their life forms and survival. The Court based its reasoning on the right to adequate food and the right to water, as contained in Articles 11 and 12 of the ICESCR. It argued that these were the underlying conditions of the right to life as foreseen in Article 4 of the American Convention on Human Rights.[285]

Similarly, in the *Case of the Xákmok Kásek Indigenous Community* v. *Paraguay*, the Court noted that the state in question was not supplying sufficient amounts of water to meet the minimum requirements.[286] Given this situation, the Court ordered the state to adopt immediately, periodically or permanently certain measures such as "provision of sufficient potable water for the consumption and personal hygiene of the members of the Community" and "installation of latrines or any other adequate type of sanitation system in the Community's settlement".[287]

Finally, in the *Case of Vélez Loor* v. *Panama*, the Inter-American Court of Human Rights declared that states must take the necessary measures to make sure that persons deprived of their freedom have access to sufficient and

285 IACtHR, *Case of the Sawhoyamaxa Indigenous Community v. Paraguay* (Merits, Reparations and Costs), 29 March 2006. Series C No. 146, p. 83, para. 164.

286 IACtHR, *Case of the Xákmok Kásek Indigenous Community* v. *Paraguay* (Merits, Reparations and Costs), 24 August 2010. Series C No. 214, pp. 44–45, paras. 195–196. The Court based its conclusion on the following calculus: total litres of water supplied by the state/number of the members of the community living in 25 de Febrero = N1; N1/period of time in calendar days, in which such assistance was actually provided = quantity of litres per person on a daily basis.

287 Ibid., p. 69, para. 301. In addition, in the *Yakye Axa Indigenous Community* v. *Paraguay* case, the Court explained: "Special detriment to the right to health, and closely tied to this, detriment to the right to food and access to clean water, have a major impact on the right to a decent existence and basic conditions to exercise other human rights, such as the right to education or the right to cultural identity. In the case of indigenous peoples, access to their ancestral lands and to the use and enjoyment of the natural resources found on them is closely linked to obtaining food and access to clean water. In this regard, said Committee on Economic, Social and Cultural Rights has highlighted the special vulnerability of many groups of indigenous peoples whose access to ancestral lands has been threatened and, therefore, their possibility of access to means of obtaining food and clean water". IACtHR, *Case of the Yakye Axa Indigenous Community* v. *Paraguay* (Merits, Reparations and Costs), 17 June 2005. Series C No. 125, pp. 85–86, para. 167.

healthy drinking water for their daily and individual requirements and they shall be provided with water and with toilets as are necessary for health and cleanliness.[288] The Court makes special reference to the UN General Assembly resolution on the human right to water and sanitation.[289]

d) *The UN General Assembly Resolution on the Human Right to Water and Sanitation*

Since 28 July 2010, the human right to water and sanitation has been expressly recognized both as a fundamental human right and a legal norm by virtue of United Nations General Assembly Resolution 64/292. This resolution can be considered a source of international law since it recognizes a right to all individuals, empowering them with a certain capacity and the corresponding obligation of the states composing the international community.[290]

Only certain resolutions of an international organization are sources of international legal norms. These groups of resolutions, which have the capacity to create new legal norms within the international legal order, amount to a *species* within the *genus* of all the existing resolutions of international organizations.[291] In order to be a source of international legal norms, they must: (a) Amount to an expression of will of an international organization with sufficient capacity.[292] The organization in question would be endowed with such capacity by virtue of its constituent treaty or statute; (b) The expression of will must not be conditioned on the consent of another subject of international law. This means that it does not depend on the consent of the member states of the organization; (c) It must tend to create a legal norm within the international legal order. Legal norms can appear in the form of prescriptions, e.g., rules prescribing a certain conduct as allowed, prohibited or mandatory, and definitions.[293] In either form, these norms encompass a modification

288 IACtHR, *Case of Vélez Loor* v. *Panama* (Preliminary Objections, Merits, Reparations, and Costs). 23 November 2010, Series C No. 218, p. 65, para. 215.

289 Ibid., p. 66.

290 Cf. Murthy, Sh., 'The Human Right(s) to Water and Sanitation: History, Meaning, and the Controversy Over Privatization', *Berkeley Journal of International Law*, Vol. 31(1) (2013), p. 103.

291 Skubiszewski, K., 'A New Source of the Law of Nations: Resolutions of International Organisations', *in, Recueil d'études de droit international en hommage à Paul Guggenheim* (Genève: Tribune, 1968), p. 508 et seq.

292 Economides, C., 'Les actes institutionnels internationaux et les sources du droit international', *Annuaire français de droit international*, Vol. 34 (1988), p. 132.

293 Barberis, J., 'Les résolutions des organisations internationales en tant que source du droit des gens', *in*, Beyerlin, U. et al. (eds.), *Recht zwischen Umbruch und Bewahrung. Festschrift*

within the international legal order. This happens when certain behaviour is established as forbidden, authorized or compulsory, meaning when an obligation is imposed. It is also the case when a certain competence, power or right is conferred and in those cases where a right, an obligation or a certain competence is modified, maintained or annulled; (d) Finally, the expression of will must be regulated by international law.

In light of the above considerations, it can be concluded that Resolution 64/292 is the source of a legal norm recognizing "the right to safe and clean drinking water and sanitation as a human right that is essential for the full enjoyment of life and all human rights". It also "[c]alls upon states and international organizations to provide financial resources, capacity-building and technology transfer, through international assistance and cooperation, in particular to developing countries, in order to scale up efforts to provide safe, clean, accessible and affordable drinking water and sanitation for all".[294]

With regard to its voting record, Resolution 64/292 was adopted by a vote of 122 states in favor to none against, with 41 abstentions. Along this line, it is worth stressing that there were no votes against the adoption of the resolution and most of the abstentions were driven by concerns that were largely procedural in character. Furthermore, only two months after this vote took place, 17 of the abstaining states co-sponsored Human Rights Council Resolution 15/9 of September 2010, which affirms that "the human right to safe drinking water and sanitation is derived from the right to an adequate standard of living" and was adopted without a vote—thereby providing strong endorsement of these rights.[295] All of the abstaining states eventually recognized the rights to water and sanitation in other resolutions and declarations, including General Assembly Resolution 68/157 of 2013, which recognizes that "the human right to safe drinking water and sanitation is derived from the right to an adequate standard of living and is inextricably related to the right to the highest attainable standard of physical and mental health, as well as to the right to life and human dignity".

The right to water and sanitation is thus a legally binding norm for all member states of the United Nations, e.g. practically the entire international

für Rudolf Bernhardt (Heidelberg: Springer, 1995), pp. 21–39 and pp. 34–35, in particular. See also Barberis, J., *Formación del derecho internacional actual* (Buenos Aires: Ábaco, 1994), pp. 159–167.

294 United Nations, A/RES/64/292, paras. 1–2.

295 These states are: Cyprus, Armenia, Bosnia and Herzegovina, Bulgaria, Croatia, Estonia, Latvia, Lithuania, Poland, Romania, Slovakia, Denmark, Greece, Iceland, Luxembourg and the Netherlands.

community.[296] It is important to bear in mind that the General Comments of the ICESCR Committee solely impose obligations upon state parties to the mentioned Covenant in as far as they have accepted them. The same is applicable to those members of the international community who are not state parties to the ICESCR. These state parties must periodically submit reports to the Committee on the implementation of the Covenant and on the progress achieved towards the implementation of the human right to water and sanitation as inherent conditions of the right to an adequate standard of living.[297] At present, there are 160 State Parties to the ICESCR. Hence, all these states are bound by the provisions contained in the Covenant, including the right to water and sanitation as inherent to the right to an adequate standard of living.

The human right to water has been expressly recognized by international courts at a regional level, such as the Inter-American Court of Human Rights, on numerous occasions as a legal norm binding upon states.[298] The consistent, repetitive and uninterrupted *dicta* of this regional court in this respect would reveal—if not yet the existence of a general customary norm—at least that of a nascent regional customary human right to water and sanitation.[299]

It has been suggested that "there is no area of law that is not related to human rights, these rights have penetrated into all legal approaches".[300] International river and lake delimitation is no exception in this respect. In the context of territorial disputes, up to the present, no state has invoked the human right to water to reinforce its claim in support of a certain delimitation method in an international river or lake.[301] Neither are there references to the need to ensure access to water as a human right in either the preamble

296 At present, there are 193 Member States of the United Nations. The last Member to be incorporated was the Republic of South Sudan, which formally seceded from Sudan on 9 July 2011 as a result of an internationally monitored referendum held in January 2011. This state was admitted as a new Member by the United Nations General Assembly on 14 July 2011.

297 McCaffrey, S., supra, note 259, p. 103.

298 See supra, pp. [79–81].

299 Cf. the International Law Commission Special Rapporteur's *First Report on Formation and Evidence of Customary International Law*, 17 May 2013, United Nations, A/CN.4/663, pp. 36–37. See also Barberis, supra, note 293, pp. 210–212 and Barberis, J., 'Réflexions sur la coutume internationale', *Annuaire français de droit international*, Vol. XXXVI (1990), pp. 9–46.

300 Drnas de Clément, Z., 'The Humanisation of International Courts', in, *International Law: New Actors, New Concepts, Continuing Dilemmas: Liber Amicorum Bozidar Bakotic* (Leiden: Brill, 2010), p. 407.

301 Cf. Kohen & Tignino, supra, note 248, p. 97.

or the articles of boundary treaties between co-riparian states. As above described, the International Court of Justice has so far recognized in the *Frontier Dispute* (*Burkina Faso/Niger*) case that access to water resources of all the people living in the riparian villages is "a requirement". Nevertheless, and given the recent trends taking place, it would not be surprising if future judgments on the subject end up recognizing the obligation for states to ensure such access to the waters of an international fresh watercourse as a human right.

In the meantime, the universal recognition of the human right to water has indeed been key in fostering the acknowledgment of human considerations in the field of international river and lake delimitation. The more prominent role of human freshwater needs in freshwater boundary delimitation has been additionally promoted by various international legal norms with other and diverse sources of validity. Both the 2004 Berlin Rules and the UN Convention on the Non-Navigational Uses of International Watercourses provide good examples in this regard.[302] These legal norms and their correlative obligations incumbent upon states have paved the way to duly consider the need to guarantee access of local communities to the waters of boundary watercourses. They have proven to amount to key elements both in treaty interpretation on lake and river delimitation and even in the recognition of new customary norms in this regard, as advanced above. Also, they can indeed complement and reinforce the sovereignty claims of co-riparian states with relation to their international rivers and lakes.

Conclusions

There are international rivers and lakes in every region of the globe. Furthermore, 263 transboundary lake and river basins in the world cover nearly half of the land of the earth.[303] Every one of these international watercourses must have been delimited at some point, or will eventually be delimited, in accordance with a certain type of boundary line. The method of delimitation chosen will often amount to a compromise solution between the natural configuration of the river or lake in question on the one hand, and the uses envisaged by the

302 Bourquain, K., *Freshwater Access from a Human Rights Perspective* (Leiden: Martinus Nijhoff, 2008), p. 31. However, this author contends that the status of both the Berlin Rules and the UN Convention is not sufficiently clear within international water law.

303 http://www.un.org/waterforlifedecade/transboundary_waters.shtml. Accessed on 20 January 2016.

co-riparian states on the other. Due consideration of both aspects, natural and human, ensure the establishment of the best possible boundary line for each particular international watercourse. In so doing, it favours the continuing cooperation of co-riparian states.

With reference to the alleged norm that prescribes the delimitation by the *thalweg* for navigable watercourses and by the median line in cases of non-navigable watercourses, it is worth recalling the absence—in the present state of international law—of customary norms prescribing resort to a particular delimitation method over other methods. The existing methods of international river and lake delimitation amount to diverse techniques to which co-riparian states resort in distributing and circumscribing their respective territories, and, thus, the corresponding spatial spheres of validity of their legal norms. In line with this view, the boundary on a number of watercourses in French Equatorial Africa (Chad) and Sudan such as the Wadi Kaja and Wadi Asunga is established on the median line even though the said watercourses possess a *thalweg*.[304]

As a result, and given the consensual basis of the norms applicable to the subject under study, states remain free to choose the method they might consider more appropriate for the delimitation of their respective international rivers or lakes. Thus, each watercourse should be approached independently on a case-by-case basis.

In light of the recent developments of the past few years in the field of fluvial and lacustrine delimitation, and of the latest jurisrpudence on the subject analyzed throughout this monograph, it is possible to identify the existence of three distinct general legal norms applicable in the field under study.

Primarily, states delimiting their respective international watercourses are bound by the general legal norm on equitable and reasonable use. Delimitation and uses of the international watercourse go hand in hand. Trying to stipulate the application of one before the other in a successive way can be assimilated to the tale of the egg and the chicken. There is no answer to such a riddle and as such it is pointless from a normative standpoint. Along this line, it has been put forward that it is impossible to separate what falls within the scope of the delimitation of a certain watercourse from what falls within that of its utilization.[305] Therefore, a balance must be achieved between the boundary aspect and that concerning the uses of a transboundary fresh watercourse.

304 Delimitation Protocol enacted by the Boundary Commission on 21 January 1924, in application of the norm established by virtue of the Declaration of 8 September 1919 between France and Great Britain. Cf. Brownlie, supra, note 82, p. 633.

305 Forteau, supra, note 55, p. 39.

There is no hierarchy in the applicable international norms pertaining to fresh watercourse delimitation and those applicable to the uses of that watercourse. A decision will be therefore adopted on a case-by-case basis. There is no ultimate best boundary line for transboundary fresh watercourses.

Another general customary rule can be deduced from all that has been stated above on the subject of international freshwater boundaries: the right of every riparian state to have access to the watercourse which it borders. Indeed, such a norm has already been advanced in our previous work on the subject.[306] Despite the lack of doctrinal consensus in this respect, this author still believes it is an international legal norm, binding upon co-riparian states.

It has been advanced that there is no general state practice, not to mention a psychological element in this respect. Access to international watercourses has been assured and depends still today on the effective exercise of governmental power that lies at the basis of the concept of sovereignty.[307]

Nevertheless, access to water is assured in the vast majority of cases where different methods of delimitation of international rivers and lakes have been applied. Consequently, it is possible to identify the presence of a constant, general and uniform practice in this respect. It is true that some scattered and numbered examples of the adoption of the single bank boundary still remain in Latin America,[308] in Africa[309] and in Asia.[310] However, in every one of the mentioned watercourses, the state that has been excluded from it has continuously and persistently expressed its opposition to this situation.

In Latin America, whereas in the case of the San Juan River, Costa Rica recently agreed before an international court—the International Court of Justice—that the boundary line with Nicaragua was indeed the riverbank, the Court made up for the inconveniences derived from such a boundary line. Not only did the Court recognize the rights of navigation of Costa Rica over the San Juan River, it also recognized the existence of a local customary norm ensuring the fishing rights of local inhabitants for subsistence purposes. In the remainder of the above-mentioned cases, the states concerned submitted claims for the revision of the boundary line, alleging that they had not given their consent to such a system of delimitation. Moreover, these states should not have imposed on them the excuse of a previously existing objective regime. As a result, these apparent exceptions would rather confirm the existence of the

306 Querol, supra, note 17, p. 131.

307 Caflisch, supra, note 2, p. 100.

308 Supra, pp. 27–28.

309 Supra, p. 28.

310 Supra, pp. 32–33.

opposite general rule: that which prescribes the right of every riparian state to have access to the waters of the river or lake in question.

Furthermore, in the delimitation of international rivers and lakes, states must abide by their obligation to respect, protect and fulfil the realization of the human right to water of its inhabitants. The human right to water is indeed a legal norm of the international legal order and binding upon all Member States of the United Nations, which represents practically the entire international community. Its source of validity is an international legal act, a resolution of the General Assembly of the United Nations. In addition, it has been recognized as a legal norm binding upon states parties to the ICESCR as well as by numerous other treaties, which have been examined above.[311]

In addition, at least within the American continent, a nascent regional customary norm with the same content has been fostered by the *dicta* of the Inter-American Court of Human Rights, which repeatedly and consistently recognizes the existence of such a human right at both a universal level and regional level.

River and lake delimitation lies at the basis of a rational exploitation of the natural resources of the watercourses in question. It provides the international system with legal security by protecting the acquired rights of riparian states over international watercourses.[312] International boundaries in rivers and lakes are a legal creation. Their application divides in practice what was naturally unified. They are a tool which international law provides to states, to enable them to divide the spatial sphere of validity of their respective legal orders.

Among the different systems of delimitation analyzed throughout this monograph, the application of certain methods in particular, such as *condominium*, which have been quickly dismissed in the past on the ground that they are outdated or seldom used, can actually provide a suitable solution for subsisting disputes over international watercourses. Despite its apparent frailness, the underlying considerations of justice of such a system would guarantee the equitable access and use of the watercourse in question. Furthermore, the particular characteristics of enclaves, endow this physical phenomenon with a renewed attractiveness in the provision of a definite response to open conflicts over the boundaries of certain international watercourses. Its singularity could furnish efficient solutions more appropriately adapted to the

311 Supra, pp. 73–76.

312 Cf. Abi-Saab, G., 'La pérennité des frontières en droit international', *Relations internationales*, No. 64 (hiver 1990), p. 345.

specific natural configuration of those watercourses and to the uses foreseen by co-riparian states.

All of the above exposes how human considerations are presently, and more than ever before, embedded within the *corpus juris* that constitutes the international legal order. As such, they have also permeated the field of international river and lake delimitation.

List of References

Primary Sources

Burchi, Stefano (ed.), *Treaties Concerning the Non-Navigational Uses of International Watercourses: Africa* (Rome: FAO, 1995).

Burchi, Stefano, *Treaties Concerning the Non-Navigational Uses of International Watercourses: Asia* (Rome: FAO, 1995).

Burchi, Stefano, *Treaties Concerning the Non-Navigational Uses of International Watercourses*: Europe (Rome: FAO, 1993).

CEPAL (Comisión Económica para América Latina), *Los recursos hidráulicos de Argentina. Análisis y programación tentativa de su desarrollo* (Buenos Aires, 1969).

COMIP (Comisión Mixta Argentino Paraguaya del Río Paraná), *Aprovechamiento energético del Río Paraná, Documentos y tratados* (Buenos Aires, 1992), 211 p.

FAO (Food and Agriculture Organization of the United Nations), *Systematic Index of International Water Resources Treaties, Declarations, Acts and Cases, by Basin*, 2 volumes (Rome, 1984).

League of Nations, *League of Nations Treaty Series.*

Martens, Charles de, *Nouveau Recueil des Traités.*

Ministerio de relaciones exteriores y culto de la República Argentina, *Instrumentos internacionales de carácter bilateral suscriptos por la República Argentina*, 11 tomos (Buenos Aires, 1950).

Parry, C., *Consolidated Treaty Series.*

United Nations, *United Nations Convention on the Non-Navigational Uses of International Watercourses*, adopted on 21 May 1997.

United Nations, *United Nations Treaty Series.*

United Nations, *Register of International Rivers* (New York: Pergamon Press), 58 p.

Dictionaries

Dictionnaire de la terminologie du droit international, avec préface de Basdevant (Paris: Sirey, 1960).

Secondary Sources

Books and Monographs

Académie de droit international, *Droit et obligations des pays riverains des fleuves internationaux*, Centre d'Etude et de Recherche de droit international et de relations internationales (La Haye, 1990).

Adami, Colonnello V., *National Frontiers in relation to International* Law (London: Oxford University Press, 1927), 127 p.

Armas Pfirter, F.; Barberis, J. A.; Beraud, A. & Freyre, N., "Límites de la República Argentina", *Cuadernos de Derecho Internacional*, Vol. 2 (Buenos Aires: Ábaco-Depalma, 2000), 175 p.

Baquero, Lazcano, Pedro, E. & Carubini, Delia B., *Problemática jurídico internacional del Río* Paraná (Córdoba, 1982), 106 p.

Barberis, J., *El territorio del Estado y la soberanía territorial* (Buenos Aires: Ábaco, 2003), 234 p.

Barberis, J., *Los recursos naturales compartidos entre Estados y el derecho internacional* (Madrid: Tecnos, 1979).

Bernstein, Itamar, *Delimitation of International Boundaries*, Thèse de l'Institut Universitaire de Hautes Études Internationales (Université de Genève, 1974), 291 p.

Boeglin Naumovic, Nicolas, *La frontière terrestre entre le Costa Rica et le Nicaragua*, Thèse de l'Université Panthéon-Assas (Paris II) (Paris, 1996).

Boggs, S. W., *International Boundaries. A Story of Boundary Functions and Problems* (New York: Columbia University Press, 1940), 260 p.

Boisson de Chazournes, Laurence, *Fresh Water in International Law* (Oxford: Oxford University Press, 2013), 265 p.

Bourquain, K., *Freshwater Access from a Human Rights Perspective* (Leiden: Martinus Nijhoff, 2008), 258 p.

Byers, Michael, *Who Owns the Arctic? Understanding Sovereignty Disputes in the North* (Vancouver: Douglas & McIntyre, 2010), 179 p.

Byers, Michael, *International Law and the Arctic* (Cambridge: Cambridge University Press, 2013), 314 p.

Coret, Alain, *Le condominium* (Paris: Librairie Générale de Droit et de Jurisprudence, 1960), 333 p.

Del Castillo-Laborde, L., *The Rio de la Plata and Its Maritime Front Regime* (Leiden: Martinus Nijhoff, 2008), 428 p.

Garretson, A. H.; Hayton, R. D. & Olmstead, C. J. (eds.), *The Law of International Drainage Basins* (New York: Oceana Publications, 1967), 916 p.

Gonzalez Lapeyre, Edison, *La Isla de la Unión: La abandonada frontera terrestre argentina-uruguaya* (Montevideo: Zonalibro, 2013), 117 p.

Hill, Norman, *Claims to Territory in International Law and Relations* (London: Oxford University Press, 1945), 240 p.

Janusz-Pawletta, B., *The Legal Status of the Caspian Sea: Current Challenges and Prospects for Future Development* (Berlin: Springer, 2015), 176 p.

Jones, Stephen B., *Boundary-Making. A Handbook for Statesmen, Treaty Editors and Boundary Commissioners* (Washington: Carnegie Endowment for International Peace, 1945).

Labreque, Georges, *Les différends territoriaux en Amérique Latine : Jurisprudence de la Cour Internationale de Justice* (Paris: L'Harmattan, 2011), 315 p.

Lambden, D. W., *Legal Aspects of Surveying Water Boundaries* (Scarborough: Carswell, 1996), 261 p.

Lapradelle, Paul de, *La frontière*, (Paris: Les Editions internationales, 1928), 367 p.

McEwen, A. C., *International Boundaries of East Africa* (Oxford: Clarendon Press, 1971), 321 p.

Oficina de límites internacionales, *La frontera argentino-chilena. Demarcación general 1894–1906*, t. I (Buenos Aires, 1908).

Pondaven, Ph., *Les lacs-frontière* (Paris: Pedone, 1972), 451 p.

Prescott, J. R. V., *Boundaries and Frontiers* (London: C. Helm, 1978).

Querol, M., *Estudio sobre los convenios y acuerdos de cooperación entre los países de América Latina y el Caribe, en relación con sistemas hídricos y cuerpos de agua transfronterizos* (Santiago de Chile: CEPAL, 2003), 66 p.

Salman, S. M. A. & Boisson de Chazournes, L., *International Watercourses, Enhancing Cooperation and Managing Conflict*, Proceedings of the World Bank Seminar (Washington D. C., 1998), 223 p.

Salman, S. M. A. & McInerney-Lankford, S., *The Human Right to Water: Legal and Policy Dimensions* (Washington: The World Bank, 2004), 180 p.

Salman, S. M. A. & Uprety, K., *Conflict and Cooperation on South East Asia's International Rivers* (Washington: The World Bank, 2002), 217 p.

Schultess, Konrad, *Das internationale Wasserrecht*, Publikationen des Schweizer. Wasserwirtschafts-Verbandes No. 3 (Zurich, 1915), 154 p.

Sharma, Surya P., *International Boundary Disputes and International Law. A Policy-Oriented Study* (Bombay, 1976).

Société française pour le droit international (ed.), *La frontière*, Colloque de Poitiers (Paris: Pedone, 1980), 304 p.

Visscher, Charles de, *Problèmes de confins en droit international public* (Paris: Pedone, 1969), 200 p.

Weiss, N. & Thouvenin, J.-M. (eds.), *The Influence of Human Rights in International Law* (Cham: Springer, 2015), 248 p.

Winkler, I. T., *The Human Right to Water: Significance, Legal Status and Implications for Water Allocation* (Oxford: Hart Publishing Ltd., 2012), 340 p.

Wolfrom, Marc, *L'utilisation à des fins autres que la navigation des eaux des fleuves, lacs et canaux internationaux* (Paris: Pedone, 1964), 260 p.

Articles

Abi-Saab, G., 'La pérennité des frontières en droit international', *Relations internationales*, No. 64 (hiver 1990), pp. 341–349.

Alvarez Jimenez, Alberto, 'Private Rights, The Use of Maps, State Responsibility and Other Issues in the International Court of Justice's Boundary Jurisprudence', *Canadian Yearbook of International Law*, Vol. 49 (2011), pp. 177–211.

Andrassy, Juraj, 'Les relations internationales de voisinage', *Recueil des cours de l'Académie de droit international de la Haye*, Vol. 79 (1951-II).

Anyangwe, C., 'African Border Disputes and Their Settlement by International Judicial Process', *South African Yearbook of International Law*, Vol. 28 (2003), pp. 29–58.

Armas Barea, C. A., 'El tratado del Río de la Plata y su Frente Marítimo', *Revista de derecho internacional y ciencias diplomáticas*, Vol. 25 (1973/74), pp. 7–31.

Barberis, J. A., 'El aprovechamiento industrial y agrícola de los ríos de la Cuenca del Plata y el derecho internacional', *Derecho de la Integración*, Vol. VII, No. 16 (Julio 1974), pp. 47–84.

Barberis, J. A., 'Bilan de recherches de la section de langue française du Centre d'Etude et de Recherche de l'Académie', *in*, *Droit et obligations des pays riverains des fleuves internationaux*, Centre d'Etude et de Recherche de droit international et de relations internationales, Académie de droit international (La Haye, 1990), pp. 15–57.

Barberis, J. A., 'International Rivers', *in*, Bernhardt, R. (ed.), *Encyclopedia of Public International Law*, published under the auspices of the Max Planck Institute for Comparative Public Law and International Law, Vol. 2 (Amsterdam: North Holland, 1995), pp. 1364–1368.

Barberis, J. A., 'Les résolutions des organisations internationales en tant que source du droit des gens', *in*, Beyerlin, U. et al. (eds.), *Recht zwischen Umbruch und Bewahrung. Festschrift für Rudolf Bernhardt* (Heidelberg: Springer, 1995), pp. 21–39.

Barberis, J. A., 'Quelques considérations sur le condominium en droit international public', *in*, Kohen, Marcelo G. (ed.), *Promoting Justice, Human Rights and Conflict Resolution Through International Law: Liber Amicorum Lucius Caflisch* (Leiden: Martinus Nijhoff, 2007), pp. 673–684.

Barberis, J. A., 'Un precedente poco conocido sobre la aplicación del uti possidetis a un río limítrofe que cambia de curso', *Anuario de Derecho Internacional* (Universidad de Navarra), Vol. X (1994), pp. 61–82.

Bauer, Konrad, 'Grenzen an Straβenbrücken uber Grenzflüsse', *Zeitschrift für Wasserrecht*, Vol. 15(2) (1976), pp. 259–266.

Bersin, A., 'Lines and Flows: The Beginning and Ends of Borders', *Brooklyn Journal of International Law*, Vol. 37 (2011–2012), pp. 389–406.

Blatter, J., 'Lessons from Lake Constance: Ideas, Institutions and Advocacy Coalitions', *in*, *Reflections on Water: New Approaches to Transboundary Conflicts and Cooperation* (Cambridge, MA: MIT Press, 2001), pp. 89–122.

Bochmann, M. & Hensel, P., 'Peaceful Management of International River Claims', *International Negotiation*, Vol. 14 (2009), pp. 393–418.

Boeglin Naumovic, N., 'De l'usage des cours d'eaux internationaux comme frontières', *in*, Boisson de Chazournes, L. & Salman, M. A. S. (eds.), *Water Resources and International Law* (The Hague: Hague Academy of International Law & Martinus Nijhoff, 2005), pp. 133–165.

Bouchez, L. J., 'The Fixing of Boundaries in International Boundary Rivers', *International & Comparative Law Quarterly*, Vol. 12(3) (1963), pp. 789–817.

Caflisch, L., 'Essai d'une typologie des frontières', *Relations internationales*, No. 63, (automne 1990), pp. 265–293.

Caflisch, L., 'Règles générales du droit des cours d'eaux internationaux', *Recueil des cours de l'Académie de droit international de la Haye*, Vol. 219 (1989-VII), pp. 12–225.

Caflisch, L., 'Essai de typologie des frontières fluviales', *in*, Aurescu, B. & Pellet, A., *Actualité du droit des fleuves internationaux* (Paris: Pedone, 2010), pp. 17–27.

Caflisch, L., 'Essai de typologie des frontières fluviales', in, Aurescu, B. & Pellet, A, 'The Law of International Waterways and its Sources', MacDonald, R. St. J. (ed.), *Essays in Honour of Wang Tieya* (Great Britain: Kluwer Academic Publishers, 1993), pp. 115–129.

Castillo Daudi, M., 'La protección y preservación de los cursos de agua internacionales', *Anuario de Derecho Internacional*, Vol. XV (1999), pp. 115–158.

Clemence, Phillipe, 'La prise en compte des îles', *in*, Aurescu, B. & Pellet, A., *Actualité du droit des fleuves internationaux* (Paris: Pedone, 2010), pp. 41–51.

Cordeiro, Newton V., 'Environmental management issues in the Plata Basin', *in*, Biswas, Asit K., et al. (eds.), *Management of Latin American River Basins: Amazon, Plata and São Francisco* (Tokyo: United Nations University Press, 1999), pp. 148–173.

Cristobal-Martes, A., 'La navegación de los ríos internacionales con especial referencia a Venezuela', *Temis: revista de ciencia y técnica jurídicas*, Nos. 29–32 (1971), pp. 41–91.

Dioukhane, Abdourahmane, 'Les problèmes de succession d'Etats dans l'affaire de la détermination de la frontière maritime entre la Guinée-Bissau et le Sénégal', *in, State Succession: Codification Tested against the Facts* (The Hague: Martinus Nijhoff, 2000), pp. 579–607.

Dipla, H., 'Le tracé de la frontière sur les lacs internationaux', *in*, Zacklin, R., & Caflisch, L. (eds.), *The Legal Regime of International Rivers and Lakes* (The Hague: Martinus Nijhoff, 1981), pp. 247–306.

Dipla, H., 'Le tracé de la limite sur les lacs internationaux', *Annuaire suisse de droit international*, Vol. XXXVI (1980), pp. 9–74.

Dipla, H., 'Les règles de droit international en matière de délimitation fluviale: remise en question?', *Revue Générale de Droit International Public*, t. 89, no. 3 (1985), pp. 589–624.

Drnas de Clément, Z., 'The Humanisation of International Courts', *in, International Law: New Actors, New Concepts, Continuing Dilemmas: Liber Amicorum Bozidar Bakotic* (Leiden: Brill, 2010), pp. 397–408.

Forteau, Mathias, 'Délimitation à la rive, au thalweg, au milieu du chenal', *in*, Aurescu, B. & Pellet, A., *Actualité du droit des fleuves internationaux* (Paris: Pedone, 2010), pp. 29–39.

Frowein, Jochen Abr., 'Lake Constance', *Encyclopedia of Public International Law*, published under the auspices of the Max Planck Institute for Comparative Public Law and International Law under the direction of Rudolf Bernhardt, Vol. 3 (1997), pp. 116–119.

Galea, Ion, 'La pratique des délimitations sur le Danube', *in*, Aurescu, B. & Pellet, A., *Actualité du droit des fleuves internationaux* (Paris: Pedone, 2010), pp. 77–84.

Gledistsch, Kristian, 'Rivers as International Boundaries', *Acta Scandinavica Iuris Gentium*, Vol. 21 (1952), pp. 15–32.

Griffiths, D. N., 'What's in a Name: Take the Legal Regime in the Caspian Sea (or Lake)', *Ocean Yearbook*, Vol. 23 (2009), pp. 161–192.

Gros Espiell, H., 'Le traité relatif au Rio de la Plata et la façade maritime', *Annuaire français de droit international*, Vol. 21 (1975), pp. 241–249.

Irmscher, T. M., 'Enclaves', *in, Encylopedia of Public International Law*, www.opil.ouplaw.com/home/EPIL.

Jimenez, Heidi, 'International Boundaries', *Thesaurus Acroasium*, Vol. XIV (1985), pp. 755–767.

Kanska, K. & Manko, R., 'Shifts in International Boundary Rivers', *Polish Yearbook of International Law*, Vol. 26 (2002–2003), pp. 135–155.

Kirschner, A. & Tiroch, K., 'The Waters of the Euphrates and Tigris: An International Law Perspective', *Max Planck Yearbook of United Nations Law*, Vol. 16 (2012), pp. 329–394.

Kohen, Marcelo & Tignino, Mara, 'Do people have rights in boundaries' delimitations?', *in*, Boisson de Chazournes, L. et al. (eds.), *International Law and Freshwater: The Multiple Challenges* (Cheltenham: Edward Elgar Publishing Ltd., 2013), pp. 95–122.

Le Besnerais, Jean-Marie, 'Les fleuves et lacs internationaux en Amérique Latine. Le droit fluvial latino-américain', *Notes et Études Documentaires, Problèmes d'Amérique Latine*, Vol. XLV (1977), pp. 73–92.

Marquez Carrasco, María del Carmen, 'Régimes de frontières et autres régimes territoriaux face à la succession d'Etats', *in*, Eisemann, M. & Koskenniemi, M. (eds.), *State Succession: Codification Tested against the Facts* (The Hague: Martinus Nijhoff, 2000), pp. 493–577.

McCaffrey, S., 'The Human Right to Water', *in*, Brown Weiss, E.; Boisson de Chazournes, L., & Bernasconi-Osterwalder, N. (eds.), *Fresh Water and International Economic Law* (New York: Oxford University Press, 2005), pp. 93–115.

McDermott Hughes, David, 'Water as a Boundary: National Parks, Rivers, and the Politics of Demarcation in Chimanimani, Zimbabwe', *in*, Blatter, Joachim & Ingram,

Helen (eds.), *Reflections on Water. New Approaches to Transboundary Conflicts and Cooperation* (Cambridge, MA: MIT Press, 2001), pp. 266–293.

Miron, Alina, 'Les problèmes de délimitation posés par les deltas', *in*, Aurescu, B. & Pellet, A., *Actualité du droit des fleuves internationaux* (Paris: Pedone, 2010), pp. 61–76.

Mukhar, Rose M., 'The Jordan Basin and the Mountain Aquifer: The Transboundary Freshwater Disputes Between Israel, Jordan, Syria, Lebanon and the Palestinians', *Annual Survey of International and Comparative Law*, Vol. 12 (2006), pp. 59–85.

Müller, Andreas, 'The Delimitation of Boundary River Waters', *Thesaurus Acroasium*, Vol. XIV (1985), pp. 663–672.

Murthy, Sharmila L., 'The Human Right(s) to Water and Sanitation: History, Meaning, and the Controversy Over Privatization', *Berkeley Journal of International Law*, Vol. 31(1) (2013), pp. 89–149.

Nys, Ernest, 'Rivières et fleuves frontières—La ligne médiane et le thalweg. Un aperçu historique', *Revue de droit international et de législation comparée*, 2ème Série, t. III (1901), pp. 75–88.

Paulson, Jan, 'Boundary Disputes Into the Twenty-First Century: Why, How ... and Who?', *American Society of International Law Proceedings*, Vol. 95 (2001), pp. 122–128.

Pellet, Alain, 'Les problèmes posés par l'alluvionnement', Aurescu, B. & Pellet, A., *Actualité du droit des fleuves internationaux* (Paris: Pedone, 2010), pp. 53–60.

Querol, M., 'Rethinking International Rivers and Lakes as Boundaries', *in*, Boisson de Chazournes, L. & Salman, M. A. S. (eds.), *Water Resources and International Law* (The Hague: Hague Academy of International Law & Martinus Nijhoff, 2005), pp. 97–132.

Querol, M., 'The Human Right to Water and Sanitation: The Challenges of Its Application in Latin America', *in*, Rey Caro, E. & Rodriguez de Taborda, M. C. (eds.), *Estudios de Derecho Internacional en Homenaje a la Dra. Zlata Drnas de Clément* (Córdoba: Advocatus, 2014), pp. 757–786.

Ranjeva, Raymond, 'Nouveaux aspects du droit des frontières en Afrique à la lumière de la jurisprudence de la Cour Internationale de Justice', *in, The International Legal System in Quest of Equity and Universality—Liber Amicorum Georges Abi-Saab* (The Hague: Martinus Nijhoff Publishers, 2001), pp. 603–607.

Rossi, Christopher R., '*Jura Novit Curia?* Condominium in the Gulf of Fonseca and the "Local Ilusion" of a Pluri-State Bay', *Houston Journal of International Law*, Vol. 37(3) (2015), pp. 793–840.

Ruiz Fabri, H., 'Règles coutumières générales et droit international fluvial', *Annuaire français de droit international*, Vol. 36 (1990), pp. 818–842.

Sadigov, Z., 'Legal Issues of the Status and Territorial Division of the Caspian Sea', *The Journal of International Maritime Law*, Vol. 11 (2005), pp. 372–375.

Samuels, J. H., 'Condominium Arrangements in International Practice: Reviving an Abandoned Concept of Boundary Dispute Resolution', *Michigan Journal of International Law*, Vol. 29 (2008), pp. 727–776.

Sand, Peter H., 'Lake Chad', *Encyclopedia of Public International Law*, published under the auspices of the Max Planck Institute for Comparative Public Law and International Law under the direction of Rudolf Bernhardt, Vol. 3 (1997), pp. 113–116.

Sauser-Hall, Georges, 'L'utilisation industrielle des fleuves internationaux', *Recueil des cours de l'Académie de droit international de la Haye*, t. 83 (1953-II), pp. 465–586.

Schlag, Martin, 'Die österreichische Bundesgrenze auf dem Bodensee', *Austrian Journal of Public International Law*, Vol. 43 (1992), pp. 241–266.

Schröer, Friedrich, 'Zur völkergewohnheitsrechtlichen Grenzregelung an Grenzgewässern', *Zeitschrift für Wasserrecht*, Vol. 12(2) (1973), pp. 78–84.

Schroeter, F., 'Les systèmes de délimitation dans les fleuves internationaux', *Annuaire français de droit international*, Vol. 38 (1993), pp. 948–982.

Schroeter, F., 'La délimitation des lacs internationaux : essai d'une typologie', *Annuaire français de droit international*, Vol. 40 (1995), pp. 910–929.

Valladao, H., 'Frontières internationales en Amérique Latine', *Thesaurus Acroasium*, Vol. XIV (1985), pp. 135–144.

Villiger, Mark E., 'Lake Geneva', *Encyclopedia of Public International Law*, published under the auspices of the Max Planck Institute for Comparative Public Law and International Law under the direction of Rudolf Bernhardt, Vol. 3 (1997), pp. 119–120.

Jurisprudence

Arbitral Awards

Chamizal Case, Arbitral Award of 5 June 1911, *Reports of International Arbitral Awards*, Vol. XI, p. 309.

Argentina/Chile Frontier Case, Arbitral Award of 9 December 1966, *Reports of International Arbitral Awards*, Vol. XVI, pp. 109–182.

Controversia sobre el recorrido de la traza del límite entre el Hito 62 y el Monte Fitz Roy (*Laguna del Desierto*), Argentina/Chile, Tribunal Arbitral Internacional, Sentencia del 21 de octubre de 1994.

Solicitud de revisión e interpretación en subsidio planteada por Chile respecto de la Sentencia del 21 de octubre de 1994, Argentina/Chile, Tribunal Arbitral Internacional, Sentencia del 13 de octubre de 1995.

Guyana v. Suriname, Arbitral Award of 17 September 2007, p. 1. (www.pca-cpa.org).

The Government of Sudan/The Sudan People's Liberation Movement/Army (*Abyei Arbitration*), Arbitral Award of 22 July 2009, p. 1 (www.pca-cpa.org).

Indus Waters Kishenganga Arbitration (*Pakistan v. India*), Arbitral Award of 20 December 2013, p. 1 (www.pca-cpa.org).

Bay of Bengal Maritime Boundary Arbitration (*Bangladesh v. India*), Arbitral Award of 7 July 2014, p. 1 (www.pca-cpa.org).

International Court of Justice

Land, Island and Maritime Frontier Dispute (*El Salvador/Honduras: Nicaragua intervening*), *Merits, Judgment, I.C.J. Reports 1992*, p. 351.
Kasikili/Sedudu Island (*Botswana/Namibia*), *Judgment, I.C.J. Reports 1999*, p. 1045.
Land and Maritime Boundary between Cameroon and Nigeria (*Cameroon* v. *Nigeria: Equatorial Guinea intervening*), *Judgment, I.C.J. Reports 2002*, p. 303.
Frontier Dispute (*Benin/Niger*), *Judgment, I.C.J. Reports 2005*, p. 90.
Territorial and Maritime Dispute between Nicaragua and Honduras in the Caribbean Sea (*Nicaragua v. Honduras*), *Judgment, I.C.J. Reports 2007*, p. 659.
Dispute regarding Navigational and Related Rights (*Costa Rica* v. *Nicaragua*), *Judgment, I.C.J. Reports 2009*, p. 213.
Pulp Mills on the River Uruguay (*Argentina* v. *Uruguay*), *Judgment, I.C.J. Reports 2010*, p. 14.
Frontier Dispute (*Burkina Faso/Niger*), *Judgment, I.C.J. Reports 2013*, p. 44.
Certain Activities carried out by Nicaragua in the Border Area (*Costa Rica* v. *Nicaragua*) *and Construction of a Road in Costa Rica along the San Juan River* (*Nicaragua* v. *Costa Rica*), *Judgment of 16 December 2015*, p. 1 (www.icj-cij.org).

www.ingramcontent.com/pod-product-compliance
Lightning Source LLC
Chambersburg PA
CBHW031331230926
51848CB00001B/184
* 9 7 8 9 0 0 4 3 3 7 9 2 3 *